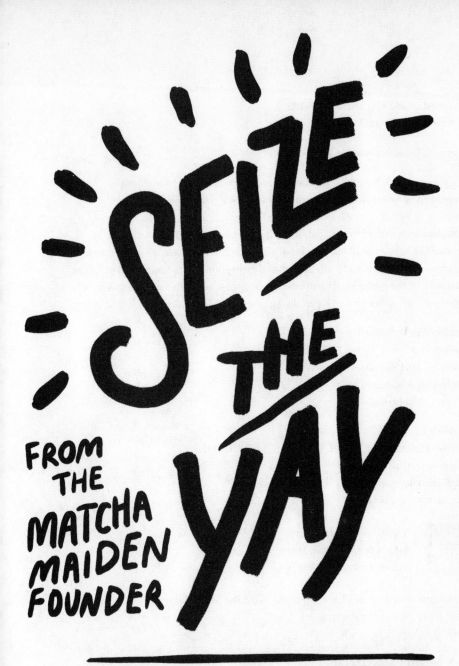

SEIZE THE YAY

FROM THE MATCHA MAIDEN FOUNDER

SARAH DAVIDSON

murdoch books

Sydney | London

Published in 2020 by Murdoch Books,
an imprint of Allen & Unwin

Murdoch Books Australia
83 Alexander Street, Crows Nest NSW 2065
Phone: +61 (0)2 8425 0100
murdochbooks.com.au
info@murdochbooks.com.au

Murdoch Books UK
Ormond House, 26–27 Boswell Street, London WC1N 3JZ
Phone: +44 (0) 20 8785 5995
murdochbooks.co.uk
info@murdochbooks.co.uk

A catalogue record for this
book is available from the
National Library of Australia

A catalogue record for this book is available from the British Library
ISBN   9 781 76052 587 3 Australia
ISBN   9 781 91163 292 4 UK

Cover design by Alissa Dinallo
Text design by Susanne Geppert
Typeset by Midland Typesetters, Australia
Printed and bound in Australia by Griffin Press

The paper in this book is FSC® certified.
FSC® promotes environmentally responsible,
socially beneficial and economically viable
management of the world's forests.

For my wonderful mum, Elizabeth; husband, Nic;
brother, Alexander; and aunties Judy and Di,
who taught me everything I know about
seizing my yay and make life such a pleasure to live.

And for our beautiful Golden Retriever, Paul, who kept me
company every single day of writing this.

Contents

Foreword

Lisa Messenger

I'm not entirely sure when I first met Sarah, but every early encounter with her was like being enveloped in a big bubble of happiness, positivity and joy. I've since learned that not only does Sarah make you FEEL fabulous every time you connect, but she's also a super-smart cookie. Everything she says or, in the case of this book, writes, is also super smart; it's raw and relatable, plus there's a delicious side of wit thrown in for good measure. As the book title suggests, Sarah is the epitome of YAY!

Relationships take time. We're all busy people. But there are those who, over the years, just chip away, in the best possible sense, at your soul. In our case, Sarah started reading *Collective Hub* and engaging from afar a few years before she properly made herself known to me. She attributes *Collective Hub* for helping her be brave enough to jump from law into her first business, Matcha Maiden – something I didn't learn until several years later.

In 2016, we were both invited to speak at Colour & Coconuts' Wellness Festival, where we finally connected in person. From there, we dipped in and out of each other's spheres until we totally fell in love and became firm friends – for what I believe will be for life.

There have been lots of firsts with Sar and I, and over the years we've developed a pretty special relationship. I was fortunate enough to be one of the first guests on her *Seize the Yay* podcast. And, after years of people hounding me about doing my own podcast, Sarah was the one who finally convinced me to launch my podcast, *Hear* me RAW; I have her to thank for the title!

In early January 2020, Sar and I bunkered down in my holiday home in Bangalow along with our mutual friend Samantha Gash. The plan was to have a girly holiday and chill out, something we entrepreneurs don't know how to do very well. Instead, Sar, Sammy and I, devasted by the bushfires ravaging our nation, found ourselves accidentally at the forefront of running significant campaigns to help the victims of the fires. It's a moment in time I'll never forget – definitely another first – and one that connected us to the community and to each other on a level I'm sure we'll not experience again soon.

I've long been a big believer that to do good business you need to have business acumen, but you also need to have loads of empathy, heart and human connection, AND you need to be able to laugh at yourself and have fun. That's why *Seize the Yay* is a concept I fell in love with from day one. As a storyteller, Sarah can weave in the all-important messages about how to survive our crazy fast-paced life in a way that's both relatable and attainable no matter where you are on your business journey.

As you read this book you'll start to recognise, and no doubt fall in love with, the smart, quirky and unique way that Sarah delivers age-old concepts; packaging them in a fun and easily digestible form.

'We can't control what comes at us, but we can control how we respond' is something I'm known to say daily and this belief is at the core of my being; it's also part of Sarah's DNA. As we've connected more personally and our friendship has deepened, I've come to know of her battle scars – she's been through a lot. Sarah takes it all in her stride and responds every single time with dignity, grace and YAY! She's woven her story selflessly into this book, allowing us to learn about mindset, attitude and how and how the life you dream of hinges on your ability to master these two things.

Seize the Yay is filled with Sarah's wisdom as well as the knowledge she's gleaned from the many extraordinary thought leaders she's encountered, learned from and connected with. Some of my little rituals, routines, and strategic game plays for success are included. You'll also find lessons from the likes of Gary Vaynerchuk, Laura Brown and many others who Sarah has interviewed on her chart-topping podcast.

Over the past few years, Sarah has come into her own as an entrepreneur. As happens for so many of us, what started on a whim has blossomed into a multi-pronged, very clever ecosystem of several businesses and product offerings across a number of platforms. Sarah Davidson can definitely hold her own in the entrepreneurial arena, and she is one to watch!

No matter what stage of business you're in, a book like this is gripping from start to finish. Anyone can write a theoretical textbook description of how to find things that light you up inside or outside of work, but when you've lived it day in and day out, there's a relatability that shines through. I've had my business for over 19 years, but as I read, I found myself nodding my head in agreement to so many of Sarah's points, having both aha moments and thinking *Gosh, I know that. Why have I forgotten to put it into practice?* It doesn't matter what stage of life or career we're in; I believe we should always be open, seeking and learning from everyone and every situation. This book delivers goodness page after page. It's like a best friend in your pocket and the essential go-to for every human in this modern, rapidly changing world.

– Lisa Messenger, Founder and
Editor-in-Chief, Collective Hub

Introduction

When you fancy yourself a hotshot young mergers and acquisitions lawyer, you never expect to find yourself sweating up a storm in a hot, stuffy commercial kitchen late at night wearing nothing but underwear, a tatty shower cap and disposable gloves. Yet there I was in all my glory, standing next to my then-boyfriend (now-husband), Nic, surrounded by plastic ziplock bags, digital scales, a heat sealer and mountains of precious, delicate powder.

Although I often describe that moment as resembling something out of *Breaking Bad*, this isn't a story about how I went on to become a drug kingpin (or queenpin). Rather, it's a tale of how an ancient superfood unexpectedly changed our lives forever. In our tiny makeshift production line, Nic and I were weighing out and bagging up portions of pure Japanese matcha green tea powder to sell through our hastily put together online store. This was the oh-so glamorous beginning of our entrepreneurial dream.

Fast forward six roller-coaster months, and our little hobby had taken off beyond our wildest expectations, pushing me to say goodbye to a thriving career in corporate law to work full-time on what we could officially call our start-up business, Matcha Maiden. And so, with no relevant qualifications or experience in food, manufacturing or selling a physical product, and despite having no financial backer or even a proper business plan, Nic and I decided to go all-in and I walked away from the safety net of a stable wage and a five-year plan. This spontaneous and drastic change in direction challenged every part of the highly organised, certainty-loving, risk-averse person I *believed* myself to be at that time. But the years since have revived the other side of me – the wildly creative, adventurous and playful side. I'd had these qualities since childhood; I just hadn't realised I'd allowed them to slowly slip away.

That once-terrifying leap away from what I *thought* I wanted has revolutionised every area of our lives. Having reconnected with my creative tendencies and great love of puns, I fondly refer to my ensuing (and radical) transformation as going from A-type to 'yay-type' and getting back in touch with the things that truly make me 'yay'. These days, the question I am asked most often is whether it was hating my job that caused me to leave law, as it is for many others who take a big leap between careers. Instead, and perhaps more worryingly in hindsight, I was simply 'fine' or 'okay' in my legal career – blindfolded by the gratification of productivity and my appreciation for having a respectable, stable job in a very tough market. The next question I'm usually asked is if it was scary to jump towards something so foreign and speculative. It was, but I think it's far scarier to think that I could have been too comfortable and grateful in that job to ever consider anything else. I still get goosebumps when I think of how I might have just settled for okay and never investigated what else was possible or how much better things could be.

I've realised through my journey that people generally won't make a change in their life unless they are actively unhappy. When certain boxes are ticked, we tend not to ask any further questions. While the age-old saying *carpe diem* (seize the day) absolutely has its merits when it comes to kicking us into gear, this mindset left me vulnerable to the glorification of busy. I hopped on what I call the 'productivity hamster wheel' in my career, where I mistook movement for direction and productivity for happiness.

It can be a wonderful thing to seize every opportunity afforded you, but not if they aren't the right ones for you. If they don't get you any closer to where you want to be, or if they distract you from asking yourself where that is in the first place, as in my case, then they aren't the right opportunities for you. Yet this is how I spent the first few years of my working life: seizing the directionless (albeit objectively successful) day but entirely disconnected with what I now call my yay.

It took a momentous happy accident to lead us to start Matcha Maiden and reintroduce me to the immense feeling of excitement and fulfilment that I now get through doing work that is creative, people-focused and dynamically fast-paced. Starting this new business (plus two others and a podcast since then) highlighted for me how law, by contrast, was not igniting my passions or strengths, and gave me the drive to spark a similar level of reflection in others.

Even though I didn't actively dislike the work in my law career, I started to ask myself, *What's the point of running yourself into the ground to become busy, wealthy and successful if you're not also happy, engaged and fulfilled?* Though I started out measuring my progress in life through objective markers of success or financial indicators, I have now redefined all the metrics I use to evaluate where I'm at in life. I've gradually cultivated new ones based on joy, fulfilment and the delicate interplay between choice, challenge and change. I have coined this approach to life my 'seize the yay' philosophy.

Paving your pathyay

The opening poem of my podcast (also named *Seize the Yay*) includes these lines: 'Busy and happy are not the same thing, we too rarely question what makes the heart sing. We work then we rest, but rarely we play, and often don't realise there's more than one way.' Seizing your yay turns the spotlight away from the busy and productive and back on pure joy and happiness – restoring parts of the unburdened childlike sense of wonder that we somehow let go of as we grow older. So often, particularly in my case, looking back at our younger selves reveals everything we need to know about what lights us up and helps us feel whole. As adults, we let layers of obligation, societal expectation and who we *think* we should be cloud our judgment and dictate our decisions. And then, we become disgruntled and spend the rest of our life trying to strip those false layers back to find who we always were.

To be clear from the outset, I don't mean to say that corporate law (or any other corporate career) and seizing your yay are mutually exclusive; for some people, they are one and the same. My legal career provided me with the most incredible foundation for everything that has come since, but it simply struck the wrong balance between the two sides of me: my fastidious fire and the creative craziness that has dominated my personality since the great Crayon-on-the-wall graffiti incident of 1993. Though I use my transition into the business world as an example throughout this book, I promise that this isn't going to be about me convincing you to leave your job just because I left mine (unless you want it to be, of course). I found my yay in becoming an entrepreneur, but you might find your joy and creativity within your job.

You might be an *intrapreneur* who switches companies, roles or even countries in pursuit of more satisfaction or happiness. You might find joy outside your work altogether; which, as we'll discuss, is important even if you love what you do; for some, it's necessarily where they find yay. I know people who say that when they take payment or add performance metrics to their passion, it kills the joy they feel for that activity. The lessons and insights in this book apply to *any* pathway; mine is just an example of one path to joy and fulfilment.

The path to yay (or dare I say, pathyay) will necessarily look different for each of you depending on your strengths, interests and circumstances – this is what makes life so exciting. My goal in this book is to simply encourage you to actively look for it to begin with. My own experience has made me acutely aware of how easy it is to get swept up by momentum and habit, settling for 'okay'. Consequently, I'm passionate about helping others break the autopilot circuit of productivity and achievement so they can take control of their life.

I can't promise that your journey or 'way to yay', will be smooth or terribly comfortable – the best ones rarely are. Advice to just start doing more of what makes you happy sounds painfully obvious, but we are complex beings, so any kind of change will be complex, too. As we will explore, seizing the yay involves striking a delicate balance between dedicated effort and investigation on the one hand, and surrender or acceptance on the other. Happiness and fulfilment involve navigating the fine line between what *happens* to you and what you ultimately make of it – what you *choose* to do.

You will consider and invest time into figuring out how (and if) your work invigorates you. Even if you find work that you love, we'll also explore how to find joy and fulfilment outside of your productive identity because re-learning how to 'play' is a crucial element of seizing the yay. As with anything new, you may experience discomfort, changes in friendships, setbacks or failures, but I promise it will all be worth it. I have discovered that discomfort is often what makes our biggest breakthroughs possible.

When our business took off, the prospect of embarking on such a dramatic life change (even though it was for the better) sparked intense risk aversion, self-doubt and over-thinking. Writing this book was not my first impostor-syndrome rodeo. So, in the chapters that follow, we will explore in depth how to navigate the throes of self-doubt, perfectionism paralysis and the many other barriers to yay (which I call 'nay to yay'). The past few years have taught me that your scariest, most uncertain and imperfect beginnings can lead to the best moments of your life. Fear and self-doubt are simply self-preservation reflexes. If you give yourself a chance to prove it, in most cases you will find that you are wildly more capable than you could have imagined. Not knowing how things will work out leaves room for them to turn out better than you ever dreamed.

Revolutionising your mindset to allow your happiest life to become a reality is sometimes a gruelling, confronting process, but it can pay dividends beyond your wildest dreams (and I don't just mean financially). Ultimately, pushing back against what society expects of us (and what we expect from ourselves) will be scary and hard. So will resisting the many shiny things that distract us on our way to happiness, but doing this can also reveal a path you never knew you were meant to be on. Investigating what makes you feel most energised and fulfilled is an exercise in experimenting, regularly reflecting, sometimes falling, but then course-correcting as you go. By sharing my story, as well as stories from some of the people who have inspired or impacted me the most, I hope I can illustrate how non-linear and unexpected the path to happiness can be. Admittedly, I still discover new facets to my pathyay every day.

There may be many chapters in your life that don't make sense at the time or leave you feeling lost or confused, but later, when you look back on them, you'll probably be able to see that those times were crucial stepping stones towards finding your yay. Even times you feel you're going backwards or failing altogether can turn out to be transformative periods that teach you the lessons and resilience you need for whatever lies ahead. Life may not turn out exactly as you had planned or envisioned it. But, through seizing your yay, it might just turn out better.

CHAPTER 1

The formation of a funtrepreneur

Before we get to seizing *your* yay, I should probably share my own story to give you some context for the ponderings that lie ahead. The earliest of many defining 'sliding doors' moments in my life – one that formed the foundations for my stark inability to leave any opportunity unexplored (or any yay unseized, if you will) – was my adoption from Daegu City in South Korea. I spent the first six months of my life between the Eastern Child Welfare orphanage in the capital city of Seoul and a delightful local foster family until my wonderful parents flew over from Australia to adopt me. After a very lengthy and burdensome approval process, and an overwhelming flight back to Australia (my poor mum dropped me down the back of the airplane change table, which explains so much), I arrived in Melbourne on 29 August 1989 – just in time for my maternal grandfather's birthday.

My ensuing perception of myself as a bit of a gift to the family lasted about four years, until my run as an only child was broken by the arrival of my younger brother, Alexander. Though born into a different biological family, like me, Alexander was adopted from the same orphanage in Seoul at six months old. Koreans believe that the child picks the family, not the other way around, and we were absolutely meant for each other; we even share the same birthday. Though a new sibling seemed like a major inconvenience to me at first, we quickly became inseparable. My parents had a lengthy, well-considered list of names ready for his arrival, but it was four-year-old me who obnoxiously announced that I wouldn't call him anything other than 'Alexander'. To this day, none of us know where I got that name from, but it suits him to a tee.

I had an idyllic and nurtured childhood in a loving household, where Alex and I got to enjoy the best of both worlds: the many benefits of city life in Melbourne as well as the strong, grounding country roots of rural Victoria since both of our parents came from small country towns (although I'm not sure we appreciated the beauty of the smelly, boring countryside at the time). We were constantly surrounded by a delightful extended family who were speckled across the state and could rival the closeness of any tight-knit ethnic family. Not only were our parents incredibly supportive of all our interests and endeavours, but we were also doted on by wonderful grandparents, cousins, uncles and aunts (plus an army of honorary family members), whose love and attention supported us to explore our every interest and activity. They say it takes a village to raise a child, and I can wholeheartedly say that this was the case for me and Alex – it led to who we are today.

Nowadays, my entirely Caucasian, country-bumpkin parents and my entirely Asian appearance generally give away my adopted status immediately, and of course it forms an important part of our heritage. However, adoption doesn't come up in conversation nearly as much as you might think. That's not because I'm uncomfortable with it; I never shy away from a chat or an overshare, as you'll discover. Being adopted has certainly given my brother and me unique cultural identities and presented us with both benefits *and* challenges along the way. You can only imagine the fun I've had turning up at interviews where my very Anglo name has preceded me.

Because adoption has been an infinitely positive experience in our situation, I actually sometimes forget about it.

Particularly as I have no memory of the parts that may have been disruptive or upsetting. (I mean, who remembers their life from birth to six months old?) So I don't view it as a defining trauma or the hardship that some might assume. Instead, being adopted has given me a great appreciation for how singular decisions or events can dramatically change our life's trajectory. Though I didn't personally choose my adoption, it made me consider that perhaps other transformative sliding doors moments in life *could* be a conscious choice.

Being adopted has left me acutely aware of how easily we can coast through life without exploring how different (and better) things could be. This realisation helped me develop the drive to make the most of every opportunity afforded me, and to help spark in those around me that excitement and sense of possibility. So, as we proceed, this might provide context for my lifelong eagerness and over enthusiasm (even for things I turn out not to like). Please also enjoy the unique cultural challenge of envisioning me, your narrator – a fully blown Asian woman – telling her story in the excitable words of the country-bumpkin Aussie bogan she grew up to be.

From arabesques to advocacy

It emerged very early on that I was equal parts nerd-burger bookworm and crazy, arty-farty performer kid. This contrast in my personality and interests continued to express itself all the way through primary school to my university years (and beyond). There's pretty much no extracurricular activity or committee I haven't been a part of. I cried when I came home from my first day of school because the teachers hadn't given us any homework and continued to complain every day that didn't involve some kind of academic rigour or stamp of achievement. But then I'd also arrange elaborate concerts for the family, and ended up dancing professionally with the Australian Ballet School until the middle of high school, when I discovered that boys and parties were more fun than training.

I'm skating over a lot of detail here, but sandwiched between my conscientious childhood and high-achieving university years was an uncharacteristically rebellious, wild phase comprised of lots of wagging school, drinking UDLs at 'gatherings' and all sorts of other teenage mischief that I won't commit to writing. Thank goodness social media was largely unheard of at that point in time; the evidence died along with my obsessions with Champion jumpers and low-rise jeans.

Though dealing with the chaos caused by my developing adolescent brain probably took years off my mum's life, she will attest that the misadventures of youth don't preclude any later yay-seizing. Not all chapters of your way to yay will make the highlight reel. Luckily, I outgrew my hideously embarrassing gangster phase just in time for Year 12, which I completed at Mac. Robertson Girls' High School, a selective girls' school. The rigorous academic environment and wonderful teaching staff were enough to coax my inner nerd back out, along with a surprisingly high result that allowed me to enrol in a double degree with a scholarship at Monash University.

Without really knowing much about what life after high school entailed or the direction I wanted to pursue, I chose to study arts and law in order to satisfy both the artistic and the analytical sides of my personality. When I finished my degree years later, I still found myself in that incredibly common position of not knowing what I wanted to be 'when I grew up' or about the scope of jobs that existed out there in the real-life workforce. So, after a process of deduction, pursuing law seemed the best option to keep as many doors open as possible. I was fortunate to secure a graduate position at a top-tier international law firm in Melbourne straight out of university, for which I was especially grateful given the post-GFC climate into which I graduated. No matter what happened, I knew that qualifying as a lawyer would never be a disadvantage, and would give me broad, transferable skills down the track.

Things have changed now, but for my cohort, it was common to try to lock in your graduate legal position years before you would ultimately start. My pathway from work experience to internship (called 'clerkship') to full-time law graduate was pretty clearly set out from early on in my university years. I just followed in the footsteps of friends in years above me. From there, the progression was mapped out: junior to senior associate, then all the way up the chain to partner. I very quickly became wrapped up in the safety of the five- to ten-year plan. Though I didn't necessarily expect that I would be a lawyer forever, I also hadn't ruled out that this could be my long-term pathway. So, suit-clad in a top-floor office in the middle of Melbourne, I got down to business and spent the first few years of my professional life working diligently to give myself the best chance to climb that ladder.

My match(a) made in heaven

While my story to this point might seem fairly jam-packed, I'd always been able to make room for boys. This dates way back to kindergarten, when I made my first 'boyfriend', Willy Carter, hold my hand at nap time (yep, I was an early starter). It wasn't until well into my university years, however, that I met my true match – or, as it later turned out, my true matcha. Though my infamous wild-child phase took a timely hiatus during my final year of high school, it enjoyed a solid revival during my first few years of university. It might be hard to imagine if you know me now, but I dominated many a dance floor and added 'nightclub host' to my long list of random part-time jobs. In the highly sophisticated and classy environment of Melbourne's Baroq House (back before dating apps when we had to meet people in person), I met my now-husband, Nic Davidson.

Nic would let me skip the queue at Baroq House for free (as I mentioned, I was super classy back then), but it wasn't until much later, in 2009, that he struck up a proper Facebook chat with me (the then-equivalent of sliding into my DMs) in the middle of my law exams. I played it cool and kept things low-key, but I was instantly captivated by his adventurousness and charisma. He was my polar opposite in the most exciting way: a lifelong serial entrepreneur, having run businesses his whole life and never having what he'd call a 'real job'. We'd stay up for hours chatting about all kinds of fun and nonsense. (I kept the cringe-worthy conversations for when we need a good giggle.)

While Nic was also always a bit of a nerd, learning early MS-DOS code as a kid, growing up in a sports-oriented family in Devonport, Tasmania, led him into his first real career as an international 400-metre hurdler. He trained alongside Jana Pittman, now our dear friend. An injury-related early retirement from athletics and return home from the European track and field circuit led him into a multi-venue partnership in high-end venues. This took him back to his techie roots, and he dove headfirst into the new world of digital, design, development and marketing.

Those new skills led to his entrepreneurial pivot into the comprehensive creative and digital agency he still owns today, The Bushy Creative, and, later, start-ups in helicopter-based aerial image capturing, artificial intelligence and prescriptive analytics software, matcha green tea (obviously) and tulip-based, clean beauty products called Bloomeffects. He's a Nic of all trades, if you will.

Everything about the subject matter and structure of Nic's working life was completely foreign and exciting to me in my little law bubble, and his spontaneous approach to life outside of work was even more intriguing. A movie night turned quickly into dating, which ultimately led to us becoming Facebook official, then settling down and slowly hanging up our dancing shoes and settling into parenthood of our beloved Golden Retriever, Paul. Over the next few years, Nic grew The Bushy Creative into a full-service digital agency while I finished university and jumped headfirst into life as a suit.

We embody the age-old adage that opposites attract, and our personalities have slowly rubbed off on each other in wonderful ways. Over the years, I've reigned in Nic's spontaneous chaos while he's relaxed my rigid need for certainty and planning ahead. I don't think either of us expected that our contrasting compatibility would ultimately translate into the perfect business partnership, and, over a decade later, a beautiful marriage. But, as you've already read, one of my favourite sayings is that things don't always turn out as you think they will – sometimes, they turn out better.

If Nic's ultimate life plan was to balance his crazy entrepreneurial life with a sensible, consistently well-salaried lawyer for a wife, I definitely ruined his plans a few years in by jumping into business alongside him. And so, we come to our second major sliding doors moment on my way to yay – the one that led to us starting our first business together, Matcha Maiden.

The pesky parasite that changed everything

Given the picture I've painted of my former by-the-book, conservative lawyer self, it might come as a surprise that the defining happy accident in this story had its origins in Rwanda. The Bushy Creative had been supporting a brilliant Melbourne-based charitable organisation called ygap, of which our very clever friend, Elliot Costello, was CEO at the time. ygap's 5cent campaign was collecting unused coins around Australia and directing them towards charitable projects in underprivileged communities, one of which was the Ntenyo School in the rural Muhanga District of Rwanda. Since Nic had provided all the digital and creative support for the campaign, we were both invited, along with a group of ygap's other major sponsors, on a month-long field expedition to help build classrooms and teach at the school.

While I am always at pains to emphasise that my legal career was a wonderful launch pad and I was never sitting there desperately seeking a way to leave, the fact that I jumped at the chance to go on this expedition was probably a fair indication that I had an underlying curiosity for life outside the legal world. I hadn't even been there long enough to accrue any annual leave, so I purchased a full month off before I'd hit the one-year mark – a seriously unheard of move among eager-to-please young law graduates.

Our month-long stay in Africa was absolutely worth the trouble, and every bit the transformative and eye-opening experience that you might expect. It sparked deep reflection and re-orientation for both of us. But the biggest takeaway, unfortunately, was a nasty little parasite that got an all-expenses paid trip back to Australia in my gut. This was the momentous surprise turn of events (now infamous among those that know me) that would eventually lead me away from that top-floor office towards the cafés, airplane tray tables, Ubers and other random places I now work from. What ultimately ensued sparked the beginnings of my transition from A-type to yay-type.

Upon returning home, I gave myself a grand total of half a day's buffer time to unpack and re-orientate my mind before heading straight back to work. Despite my body's very clear signs, for months I was completely oblivious to the strain my body was under, or the havoc my evil little parasite had begun to wreak on my digestion, energy levels and sleep. I've always had a naturally slender frame (one of the perks of my Asian genes), but I shed a whopping 15 kilograms in the months after visiting Africa before I realised that my body was compromised. While I consider myself reasonably intelligent, I've never been slower on the uptake than during that time. This was my introduction to the blind spot we often develop when we feel productive and fuelled by the adrenaline of being 'busy'. I was so focused on work, and so out of tune with what I really needed back then that it took a complete breakdown mid-way through a team meeting for me to appreciate that something was awry.

I remember sitting with colleagues one morning, trying to keep up with our regular morning meeting, when I noticed my heart starting to race uncontrollably, my stomach starting to clench and curious tingles shooting up my arms and legs. I spent a few minutes in staunch denial, then confusion, followed by nauseous terror that I might embarrass myself by passing out or throwing up on someone. Finally, I excused myself and rushed to the bathroom to experience what I now know was a full physiological panic attack brought on by beating my poor body into the ground.

It took me several hours spent in varying waves of panic and faintness to emerge from the bathroom – weak, dizzy and confused by this apparently sudden onset of complete depletion. I was going to the gym regularly and eating all of my green vegetables, so why had my body rudely and abruptly decided to stop cooperating with me? Of course, I headed straight to the doctor, fully expecting a quick fix of some sort and a medical certificate that I could take to work the next day before getting on with it again.

Unfortunately (but, ultimately, fortunately), it took many weeks of appointments and time off before we figured out that I had a gut parasite with a delightful side of adrenal fatigue that had been a long time in the making. It was many months before I started to make headway with my recovery, realising the back seat that my health had been taking all this time.

I was soon initiated into the wonderful world of health and wellness and I quickly became intimately acquainted with the delights of holistic nutrition, alternative medicine and this brand new, revolutionary concept called 'rest' (my grasp of which still leaves a lot to be desired). This lifestyle overhaul necessitated, among other things and much to my devastation, a complete ban on coffee and other strong stimulants – a hellish fate for a mergers and acquisitions lawyer still working long hours propped up by a hefty ten cups a day.

Just when I was becoming well enough to manage a full-time work load again, I was given an incredible opportunity to work in Hong Kong at my firm's global headquarters for a few months. This was another of the universe's many strokes of brilliance and fortuitous timing, and my expat stint in this vibrant city remains one of the most fulfilling and exciting periods of my life. It led me to discover the delights of 24-hour yum cha, mountain hiking and the life-changing answer to my coffee cravings. Enter the healthier caffeine alternative and superfood superstar that is matcha green tea.

The marvels of matcha!

If you haven't heard of matcha green tea powder, it sounds fancier and more complicated than it actually is. Matcha is simply a fine powder made from stone-ground green tea leaves. Instead of throwing out the leaves after brewing the tea, like you do with a regular green tea bag, you dissolve matcha power in the water and consume the whole leaf. Regular green tea has been hailed for its many health benefits for centuries, but in the more concentrated form of matcha, it packs up to 137 times the antioxidants of a regular cup of green tea. Antioxidants are heroes in the health world because they help prevent or slow the cell damage caused by free radicals, which are produced by the body in response to environmental or other factors that cause oxidative stress. Free radicals have been linked to all kinds of diseases and inflammatory conditions including cancer and diseases like Alzheimer's and Parkinson's.

 Matcha fast became a regular staple in my daily routine, providing me with a boost of sustained energy without sending my body into overdrive.

Matcha also contains a unique amino acid called L-theanine that allows the still reasonable amount of caffeine it contains to slowly release into your bloodstream over three to four hours, thus avoiding the spike and subsequent crash often associated with coffee. This is why it gained favour among the Zen Buddhist monks who turned to matcha for their long and focused meditation practices, and it quickly became ubiquitous in the East. When I lived in Hong Kong, matcha was offered everywhere I turned from traditional teahouses to Starbucks coffee shops. It fast became a regular staple in my daily routine, providing me with a boost of sustained energy without sending my body into overdrive.

This wondrous green powder made the perfect match(a) for my recovering body, answering my need for a decent boost of energy without disrupting my fragile adrenal system. When I started to tire of the daily matcha latte, I started to get more adventurous, adding it to smoothies, bliss balls and even baking. On our return to Australia in 2014, Nic and I were hooked, so we immediately sought a reliable local supplier so we could continue our new daily habit back home. However, after searching high and low for an affordable and accessible option, we were surprised by the lack of a decent supply, especially given the booming health and wellbeing market sweeping the country. There were alarming numbers of people suffering the flavour of spirulina for its benefits despite it tasting like a foot, so surely the much more palatable matcha powder should also be taking the world by storm? Nonetheless, and fortunately for us in the end it was only available in certain limited contexts.

At that point, our options included an exorbitantly expensive ceremonial-grade matcha in a tin from a specialty Japanese tea shop (think Christmas present for your grandparents), which even my legal salary wouldn't support on a daily-use basis. The other end of the spectrum offered a watered down, additive-filled variety sold from local Asian supermarkets – usually with no English on the label to indicate that it was actually matcha at all.

Given matcha's many incredible nutritional properties, deliciousness, and the general population's familiarity with the benefits of green tea, we couldn't understand why nobody had closed this glaring gap with a beautifully branded, Instagram-friendly, wellness-oriented matcha offering. So we turned to Google, and a few frustrated, late-night sessions in pursuit of our own personal needs led us to stumble across a delightful tea farm in Japan harvesting a seemingly perfect organic blend in the uncharted middle ground of cost-effective but premium-quality.

It seemed we had found our perfect matcha, but our bubble was quickly burst by their minimum order quantity of 10 kilograms at a hefty price of US$5000. While that sounds like an incredible amount of money at face-value, once we discovered that matcha has a 12-month shelf life, we thought that 10 kilograms of matcha powder at US$1 per serve didn't sound too bad for a couple who had come to adore it. However, when you do the math properly and realise that 10 kilos equates to nearly seven serves of matcha per day *each* for 365 days straight, you start to get a picture of the excessiveness involved. You can probably also understand the impossibility of stockpiling that much matcha comfortably in our house. Sure, we had a lot of snap-lock containers, but let's be real, we never have the right lids for those anyway. More frustrated late-night Googling failed to unearth any similar alternatives, and also started to reinforce in our minds that there was a timely and sizeable gap in the market for a direct-to-consumer, accessible and affordable matcha supplier.

So, in that completely unexpected, but exhilarating light-bulb moment, the idea to *become* that supplier and sell some of that 10 kilograms to legitimise our own purchase was spawned. Just like that, the foundations for Matcha Maiden were laid. I was instantly intrigued by the prospect of having a side hustle, as I'd occasionally fancied myself a potential future entrepreneur, albeit many years further down the track. Nic loved the service-based businesses he already owned, but he was also excited about the possibility of working with a tangible product.

All we really hoped for at the time was to cover some of the costs of our own personal supply, even if we weren't ultimately able to break even. This also gave us an excuse to spend more time together as our day jobs were making that challenging. Plus, I figured all I needed to do was to sell one single bag of the powder to be able to put it on LinkedIn that I was an 'entrepreneur' (yes, I openly admit I was a serial résumé padder back then); anything beyond that was a bonus. With this in mind, we ripped off the metaphorical business bandaid and bought our first 10 kilograms of matcha, forcing us into whatever chain of events would make our idea of on-selling a reality.

Over a weekday lunch date we furiously scribbled our ideas for names and logos on a serviette (in the most professional of inaugural meeting 'minutes'), and discussed how we could launch the relatively unknown matcha powder across the vast interwebs through Instagram and an online store. I knew I'd kept Nic around for a reason because his creative and digital skill sets proved invaluable in building the infrastructure that would bring our little idea to life. A few nights later, I sat bolt upright in the night with the name of our new project on my lips. You'll have noticed by now that I love alliteration, and we wanted a name that gave the business a personality, so our first business baby was christened 'Matcha Maiden'.

From zero to (superfood) hero

Once we had the name for our side hustle, our next, incredibly advanced step was to search 'how to start a tea business' on Google. I know that probably sounds cliché, but it's cliché for a reason: the humble Google search has delivered time and time again on our business journey, and it's an alarmingly more common start-up tool than I'd ever realised. At the very least, this initial research task helped us form a very basic list of our next key steps (and looking back, I'm reminded that all you ever need to make any dream a reality is a basic list of next key steps). By looking at existing tea products available online, we were able to identify all the things we'd need in order to deliver our product safely to the public (aka our parents and best friends).

Aside from the tea itself, our research quickly revealed that we needed something to put it in, something to seal that vessel with and then a label to go on it. It also gave us a rundown of the broader tea landscape, which encouraged our decision to sell the matcha in 70-gram portions. We weighed these out with small scales from eBay (that I suspect were intended for other purposes), portioned them in ziplock bags from Alibaba, and then sealed them with a rudimentary heat sealer from . . . Neither of us remembers where.

I cannot tell you how many times I rushed to Officeworks to print our first rounds of DIY labels. I'd head off, full of the new self-importance of a legit businesswoman, only to spend hours lining up behind university students printing their exam notes. But these delightful runarounds were squeezed in between our day jobs, so Officeworks at peak hour was all I could manage.

Our next step was to form a very primitive production line to actually get the matcha into the bags and ready to sell. Not having near enough volume to warrant a third-party packing facility (or knowing where to find one or even that they existed back then), Nic and I hired a friend's commercial kitchen to use after hours – as you've now read – to pack the matcha ourselves.

Years on, the incredible inefficiency of this set-up makes me laugh (and shudder); we'd have to pack every few days to keep up with demand, getting through less than 100 bags each time. Until we secured our first distributor, we would store the matcha there until 'dispatch' (code for one of us running to the post office in our lunch break). I'll never forget the first order that came through from someone who wasn't a supportive friend or family member. We were absolutely blown away that a stranger had paid real money for our product. But as it turned out, so many strangers had been waiting for someone to close the matcha gap that less than a week later, we had sold out completely and the Matcha Maiden journey had officially begun.

CHAPTER 2

The self-sabotage of self-doubt

Now that you're familiar with some of our backstory, let's get back to seizing *your* yay. And what better place to start this chapter than with some words on getting started? The many new beginnings Nic and I have embarked on over the past few years, including not only Matcha Maiden, but also more recently, writing this very book, have revealed to me that the hardest part of almost any endeavour is rarely its unfolding or implementation, but simply mustering up the courage to commit to it at all.

You might have picked up this book because you're dreaming up your very own side hustle or business idea, considering a dramatic life change or simply looking to new projects that will incorporate more joy into your life in smaller ways. Regardless of where you're at on your own way to yay, the very first step to making those dreams a reality will generally be the toughest one you make. Not necessarily in terms of what taking that step physically involves, but more in the mental and emotional challenge of taking it.

Enter the notorious impostor syndrome and my enduring favourite motivational quote on the destructive effect of self-doubt from American poet, writer and philosopher, Suzy Kassem: 'Doubt kills more dreams than failure ever will.' Each chapter that follows covers a different major facet of seizing your yay to build on the last as you work your way through the book. The creeping sense of self-doubt triggered by anything novel and unfamiliar is, at once, one of the most natural and common – but also destructive – human tendencies. It can send unsettling, disparaging voices through your mind, leading you to question the worthiness of your ideas, your abilities or even yourself. I suspect that this internal 'I'm not good enough' dialogue may sound very familiar to many of you. The resulting lack of confidence and uncertainty can lead to sabotaging reactions that nip dreams of all kinds in the bud before they ever have the chance to get off the ground and, ultimately, prove those limiting beliefs wrong.

You might assume that the further you progress or the more successful you become, the less you'll worry about being a fraud or otherwise unworthy but, in my experience, not even the most successful and confident people are immune from its clutches. Particularly when Matcha Maiden really started to flourish and grow, I found myself expecting to wake up with a staunch confidence that would create an impenetrable armour against impostor syndrome but (spoiler alert) that day has not yet arrived. So, for any of you struggling against self-doubt or feelings of unworthiness as you approach the new or unfamiliar, please know that you are absolutely not alone nor are those feelings and later success, fulfilment or joy mutually exclusive. Let me reassure you that you can harness and use those feelings to your advantage once you learn how to manage them.

Rather than ridding myself of self-doubt and nerves, I now interpret these feelings as healthy markers that I am invested in what I'm doing and not becoming complacent. In fact, I would worry if they ever disappeared completely. Though the distorting and unsettling whispers of impostor syndrome do, I assure you, still pop by for a cuppa at the most inconvenient of times, I'm getting better at distinguishing them from reasonable and useful self-evaluation, acknowledging their presence then simply moving on. Like any great skill, mastering your inner critic takes repeated and dedicated practice. It will, I promise, get easier with time. Even as I acknowledge my worries that this book won't be everyone's cup of tea, I also know our story has already provided varying degrees of inspiration and guidance to people. I hope that this longer expression of it can do the same, and more, for others.

The many times along this journey where self-doubt nearly toppled me have shown me the terrifying cost of letting fear scare me away from my dreams. How tragic it would be if I'd never found out what I was capable of purely because I couldn't believe it was possible. Sure, every single one of your ideas might not work. Various obstacles or bumps in the road (the 'nay to yay') might stop certain dreams of yours from coming true, but they might also redirect you to even better ones. As our story, and the stories of many successful people, demonstrates, those obstacles could mean things work out better than you ever imagined, if you just give them the chance.

Our close call: how Matcha Maiden almost didn't happen

Allow me to run you through an example of how my self-doubt very nearly sabotaged Matcha Maiden before she was even born. Reflecting on this close call years later, with the benefit of hindsight, has made me desperately passionate to help others distinguish between reasonable concerns and the fallacies of impostor syndrome. As I've mentioned, at the start, our goals for Matcha Maiden were quite conservative. At best, we envisioned it being a one-off side hustle that would allow us to sell the excess powder that we couldn't consume ourselves and recoup a bit of cash in the process. At worst, we would fail to sell anything at all, in which case our net position would be almost the same as it was if we'd never had the idea at all – so it wasn't really a 'worst case' at all. In hindsight, this was a relatively low-risk endeavour: we'd already paid for the stock, both of us were keeping our existing income streams and we were investing very little funding into the infrastructure in favour of a DIY build-your-own-website, pack-your-own-product situation.

But of course, impostor syndrome isn't remotely rational. Amid all our excitement, self-doubt crept nimbly into my mind from the beginning. Rather than focusing on the opportune gap in the market, our combined transferable skills and the fact that we had very little to lose even without those things going for us, I became consumed with the barriers, limitations and every way that things could go wrong (which, to be fair, is exactly what lawyers are trained to excel in, so my journey has involved a lot of unlearning). Among the most glaring barriers was, undoubtedly, the fact that we had absolutely no qualifications or experience in importing, manufacturing, or food.

If you are considering a similar life change or new project, I don't necessarily recommend choosing the option that's the *furthest* possible one from your strengths and experience to jump into headfirst, like we did. However, even if you do, you will find out over the coming chapters that this is still no reason why things can't work out wonderfully. In fact, sometimes the naivety and untainted perspective of being a complete outsider can actually work in your favour. But it does mean your self-doubt radar might go off with a special fervour reserved just for those full-body leaps outside of the comfort zone.

This was precisely the case the very first time I nervously pitched the idea for Matcha Maiden to a third party beyond our immediate family to get some feedback or pointers in the right direction. Nic and I were, and still are, very lucky to be surrounded by friends who also happen to be wonderful entrepreneurs and business owners who have forged a path ahead of us and shared their knowledge and resources generously many times over. The importance of who you surround yourself with in the crucial stages of a new beginning (or any time, really) is such that it has its very own chapter later in this book: 'Building your yay-bourhood'. But people whose support and guidance warrants mentioning early on are the founders of Frank Body, the coffee scrub and skincare sensation that broke the internet and catapulted Aussie businesses onto the global landscape.

Prior to founding Frank Body, three of the founders had started the copywriting and creative agency, Willow & Blake. Nic had been heavily involved in that company early on, leading us to develop a great friendship with those women and the two lads they later developed Frank Body with. In the weeks before we launched our business, I turned to one of the lovely co-founders Jess Hatzis to run our little business idea by her. I wanted to temperature check the structure of our business, as well as the name, logo and launch strategy that we had planned with someone who knew the ropes.

I'd known Jess for a couple of years by this point, and I really admired her business brain, creative vision and humility (which I have continued to admire through our years of friendship). Since the power of a good first impression is universally acknowledged, you'd think I would have pushed our idea to its most optimistic limits and put our very best foot forward when presenting Matcha Maiden to Jess. After all, this was the first external feedback we'd ever had. And yet, reading back through our Facebook conversation years later informs me that my choice first words were that I was working on 'a mere imaginary distracting time-passer at work' that probably wouldn't go much further than a daydream. Not the strongest of openers in hindsight.

Thankfully, I did mention very briefly that we had a great opportunity to be the first to market matcha in this health-focused way, as well as the many wonders and beneficial properties of the powder itself. But the bulk of my message was taken up by

a) apologising for taking up her time;
b) emphasising that I knew this was a 'terrible idea' that 'probably won't amount to anything'; and
c) retracting all of what I'd said anyway, because it wasn't worth asking about to begin with.

So strong was the intensity of my impostor syndrome that I was pre-empting our complete failure before we'd started. Now, with a more objective perspective, a bit of maturity and a lot of self-work, I can see those feelings were a natural protection mechanism – which is not, in itself, a bad thing – but, if I'd given too much weight to those feelings, they could have prevented us from starting Matcha Maiden at all.

You'll have gathered by this point that I did eventually end up emerging from the vicious sea of self-doubt so that we could start the business, and it didn't crash and burn in its first few days as I had feared. But now you also know how easily we could have scrapped the idea altogether had it not been for Jess' warm encouragement stopping me from falling over the edge. Much to our surprise, it turned out there were so many other people around the world waiting for someone to close the gap for accessibly and well-marketed matcha. Thanks to them, we somehow sold out of everything including our own personal stash of matcha powder within a mere seven days of launching our online store.

To prove how ill-equipped and unprepared we were for any kind of growth or success, we couldn't even find the original matcha tea supplier's details to re-order the product, having never anticipated that we'd need to use them again. And yet, at the time of writing, we're still here over five years later, several million serves of matcha deep, with warehouses in Australia, the United States and Europe, and supporters including Victoria's Secret Angels, elite athletes and leaders in the health and wellness industry. As I write this, the ink is barely dry on a new investment partnership opening up a bright-green future ahead. And we almost stopped ourselves ever knowing it was all possible.

Those very early stages of choosing whether to begin at all truly exemplify the theme of this chapter, and still give me the biggest rush to reflect on. It astounds me to think we could have very easily been scared off from trying and never seen how wonderful Matcha Maiden could become or what other opportunities it could lead to. This makes me passionate about helping others recognise and challenge their self-doubt reflex and have a chance at overcoming it. I don't mean to say thoughts of self-doubt should disappear altogether – I believe they are a healthy indication that I care about what I'm doing and that I haven't developed a blind spot to my weaknesses or areas for improvement. It's more that I want to illustrate the dangers of letting those thoughts dictate your decisions at the expense of your dreams. My hope is that you can learn to acknowledge them with a knowing smile, but gently push them aside and get on with things.

Strategies for dallying between 'this is shit' and 'this is great'

To help you face these kinds of inner negative chitchat, I want to share some of the strategies that have proven useful in overcoming, albeit not completely extinguishing, my self-doubt. The undeniable frontrunner of these, for me, is the impact of the company you keep. As I mentioned, this topic of building your support network or, as I like to call it, your 'yay-bourhood', gets its very own chapter later, but it warrants mentioning here, too, because a feeble inner voice, no matter how negative or overwhelming, can rarely stand up to an outer expression of positivity and affirmation from those you love and admire. The flip side of this is that an unsure and doubtful voice will strengthen if it finds itself among a choir of other voices reinforcing its negativity.

If Jess had responded to my pitch with scepticism or been disparaging about our idea, this would have fuelled my self-doubt and given it enough weight to change my decision. Matcha Maiden would have been stopped in its tracks on that very day. Instead, her reassuring, encouraging and supportive response helped quieten my fears of failure and tip the balance back towards believing we *might* actually be onto a good thing.

 A feeble inner voice, no matter how negative or overwhelming, can rarely stand up to an outer expression of positivity and affirmation from those you love and admire.

How terrifying and strange it is to think that a Facebook conversation of barely a few lines could become a crucial sliding doors moment that would make or break an entire business idea – one that ultimately changed the course of our lives completely. Yet, that's how delicate the balance between 'this is a bloody awesome idea' and 'this is a sure path to failure and humiliation' can be. Small things, like a trusted friend's support at the right moment, can make all the difference.

It turns out that giving Matcha Maiden the chance to flourish not only resulted in one successful business, but also opened up a world of subsequent brand-new beginnings that we might never have known were possible. In another signature midnight-idea-turned-business-opportunity, we opened a now world-renowned, plant-based Melbourne eatery Matcha Mylkbar in 2016 that Chris Hemsworth named his favourite café in Australia (so I can absolutely now retire). Then in 2018, I launched my human interest podcast, *Seize the Yay*, which is fast becoming a brand of its own that's drawn millions of downloads tuning in to interviews with inspirational guests such as entrepreneurs Gary Vaynerchuk, Miranda Kerr, Wim Hof, and over a hundred more. In the conception and early planning phases of both projects, that delicate balance of internal confidence was permeated once more by dreaded impostor syndrome, which sent whispers of uncertainty and irrational fears into my already overactive mind. But this time around, I was better equipped to acknowledge and set those feelings aside.

To this point, you've been hearing a lot about my experiences, but these themes are also recurring and reflected in the stories of so many others. Recently I found myself quite unexpectedly on the other side of the table (both literally and figuratively) from someone I thought would have no issues with self-doubt. The very clever and prolific Lisa Messenger, author of several books and the founder of Collective Hub, has become a dear friend of mine, and I feel very lucky to have advanced from embarrassingly excitable fangirl to good friends. We caught up for a coffee (or, should I say, matcha) to chat about life when she casually mentioned that she'd been told several times that she should start her own podcast. Though she had considered it briefly, ultimately, she had dismissed the idea and moved on.

I was immediately excited by the idea of Lisa doing a podcast – especially with Collective Hub evolving from a print magazine to a multi-channel digital empire. I agreed wholeheartedly that she would make an engaging and exciting podcast host. I was curious as to why she'd decided against it, and expected to hear a completely acceptable response about her already jam-packed schedule or interest in pursuing other projects. The very last thing I expected to hear from this incredibly talented and entrepreneurial woman was that podcasting was already a highly saturated market, with so many great shows out there to compete with. Lisa explained that she wasn't sure what she could add to the crowded landscape, let alone figure out how to get started in terms of equipment, design and production.

I immediately set about explaining not only how simple the set-up process is, but also how infinitely valuable it would be to add an audio dimension to her regular delivery of thought-provoking, inspiring content. We ended up in hysterics about the irony of me giving this advice to her; after all, she was the one who taught me (along with many others) that a highly saturated market is the perfect market to disrupt; inundation proves appetite and, because we all add our own distinctive spark to our work, no two ideas are really the same anyway.

This brings up yet another important aspect to the self-doubt dilemma: we are excellent at quelling everyone else's self-doubt but not our own. You already have every single tool you need to dispel your doubts; you probably exercise them regularly and with ease on behalf of those you love and care about yet forget them completely when it comes to yourself.

Hence why the support of those around you is so important when it comes to something as small as a Facebook conversation or coffee/matcha date, or as big as literally investing in you and your ideas. It follows that you should very carefully choose those you have around you so that, in times of need, you turn to people who will support and not crush your dreams (see chapter 5). It is still important, however, to also develop your own internal strategies to lean on at those moments when big dreams and ideas hang in the balance. As any self-work does, these strategies may take many years to curate and perfect – they have for me – but being aware that it is possible to overcome your internal impostor dialogue is a great first step.

 You already have every single tool you need to dispel your doubts.

As a side note, while I use my transition into the business world to demonstrate the pervasiveness of self-doubt, that's not to say it didn't also affect me in my legal career, too. I skated over the details of the corporate part of my career not because I was consistently confident, but simply because self-doubt affected me less in that world than when I changed careers and industries altogether. I had studied law and undergone work experience for almost seven years to prepare for my job as a lawyer, so while the learning curve was steep, I was not nearly as unprepared and bewildered as I was going into business for myself. Nonetheless, self-doubt was still a big factor for me back then, and when applying for promotions or other opportunities, I turned to books like Sheryl Sandberg's *Lean In* and Dr Lois Frankel's

Nice Girls Don't Get the Corner Office to help me push through those feelings of low confidence.

No matter what your work or whether your goal for seizing your yay is personal or professional, the discussion here applies. Above all, cultivating self-awareness and knowing yourself are what will help you move forward. The following strategies are examples of things that have worked for me and those in my network. I encourage you to experiment with these and tweak them to find what works for you.

Strategy 1: Power posing and physical confidence cues

One of the easiest and most effective ways to combat feelings of self-doubt is to redirect your focus and energy towards building confidence. While there are always external realities at play, it is often how we *perceive* those realities that has the biggest impact on how things turn out. I once believed that we are helpless victims to our feelings and thoughts, and sometimes we are. But, over time, I have learned how much more control we have over our thoughts than we think. We are not powerless to direct them. In fact, building strong pathways and strategies to combat unhelpful thought patterns is crucial.

One of the coolest strategies I regularly use is one I only

recently stumbled across. It's based on the impact of our physical behaviours and body language on our internal mental and emotional state. There are some wonderful physical cues you can turn to when you find yourself in the clutches of impostor syndrome. Back in 2016, when we were just two years into Matcha Maiden and still feeling very new, I was booked for my very first speaking gig at The Wellness Festival, put on by Colour & Coconuts in front of an audience of 500 people. This was positively enormous to me at the time (still is, in fact) as I'd never spoken to an audience for longer than five or ten minutes, let alone for an hour, which was the slot I was given on this occasion. I remember feeling manifoldly more intimidated and nervous because the line-up I was joining included women I had been admiring and fangirling over since we had started the business (if not well before): model Rachael Finch; Melissa Ambrosini, author of *Mastering Your Mean Girl* (the inner critic or voice of self-doubt being the 'mean girl'); Lisa Messenger; Julie Stevanja of athleisure disrupter Stylerunner; and Carla Oates of The Beauty Chef. I have absolutely no game face, so I made no secret of how nervous and awkward I was feeling about taking the stage when I met these wonderful women in the wings.

I will always remember getting the loveliest pep talk from Rachael, who has been a huge support throughout this whole journey. She talked to me about how nerves were completely normal and how we had been chosen to speak because we had something valuable to say. Then, just before I went on, Julie took me aside to introduce me to the beauty of the power pose, which I had never heard of before then. We stood there together for several minutes, hands on hips, shoulders pulled back and legs planted solidly shoulder-length apart like tree trunks, allowing the pose to work its magic on our confidence. I have resorted to the power pose backstage many times since then to calm the nerves and restore my confidence before a big event and think of Julie every time.

The power pose Julie and I discussed is the brainchild of Amy Cuddy, a professor at Harvard University who studies body language and the impact it has on your hormones. She talked about power posing in her TED talk, and about the psychology behind our physical body language and internal confidence. To briefly summarise, Amy's team's research looks at 'high power' and 'lower power' poses and the impact those poses have on certain hormones in our body. Low-power poses are quite closed off and guarded; they tend to be the positions we default to when we're feeling uncertain or unsure of our abilities – hunched over, arms across our bodies and physically shrinking into the space. High-power poses, in contrast, are more open, physically expansive and relaxed. These have been shown to increase feelings of power and confidence – you're physically taking more space in the room and asserting yourself.

The most well-known of these, and the one Julie so generously introduced me to, is called the 'Wonder Woman pose'. You do it by standing tall with your legs slightly apart, throwing your chest out, popping your chin up and placing your hands on your hips. Of course, this isn't a magical catch-all solution that will instantly instil miracle abilities and confidence in you by itself. It is, however, a valuable tool in the toolbox that can have a positive impact on your confidence levels.

There are many other researchers out there looking at the close links between our physical behaviours and the way they cue our emotions (as well as how others perceive us). Like many scientific papers, Amy's study has been hotly debated, particularly her original claims that power poses increased testosterone levels in the person posing by 20 per cent while decreasing the stress-hormone, cortisol, levels by 25 per cent. Amy has since published new findings, however, offering ample evidence that expansive postures can, in fact, make people *feel* more powerful by providing little 'self-nudges' to produce psychological and behavioural improvements in the moment. I won't get too science-y on you, but I mention power posing and other non-verbal cues because they can be an important strategy to help you *feel* more confident and boost self-esteem in those pivotal moments where you might otherwise crumble with self-doubt.

Through trial and error, you may find your own, completely different physical behaviours to help combat the impostor syndrome and instil confidence – one size does not fit all in the case of self-doubt quashing, confidence-building cues. One of my favourite real-life examples of using physical behaviour to enhance confidence is Lisa Messenger's pre-game strategy for speaking. She's a seriously impressive entrepreneur who can whip out a solemn game face when needed, but I absolutely love what a crazy cat she is at heart. While I'm off in a corner taking things very seriously and power posing myself into being ready to deliver a talk, Lisa is off in her corner, dancing away to a deep house playlist before every single speaking gig – more my pre-game ritual for the gym than combating self-doubt. This works so well for her that she's even released her own deep house track for shits and giggles.

Some of you might turn to energy-releasing activities like a short run, or even venture into the quirky or superstitious. Author and speaker Tony Robbins starts his presentation mornings in a freezing cold pool, while NBA star LeBron James throws chalk dust in the air before each big game and there are countless other examples among the world's best and brightest. If something works to help you feel more confident, who cares what it looks like or how 'weird' it might seem objectively? It's worth investing some time and energy into investigating the behavioural and environmental factors you can tweak to help improve or focus your mindset.

Though I hadn't encountered the power pose before Julie introduced it to me, I was already fascinated with the relationship between our physical behaviours and confidence during my corporate career. I mentioned the book *Nice Girls Don't Get the Corner Office* earlier, and it probably speaks to how much softer I was back then that Mum gifted me this book when I started at the firm to prepare me for the tougher environment (I'm a serial confrontation-avoider and self-proclaimed lover of the 'fluffy' and 'huggy'). Our physical behaviours don't just cue internal confidence, they also project outwardly, influencing the way others respond to us, which can also provide an internal confidence boost.

I highly recommend reading this book – it's full of fascinating examples and pointers. For example, nothing irks me more or reveals insecurity than a limp handshake, but I'm equally put off by an overly confident introductory shoulder dislocation. Reading this book taught me not to sit meekly at boardroom tables with my hands folded underneath, but rather to lean forward with my forearms *on* the table in order to be more actively part of the discourse. The book covers all sorts of small details and behaviours including how speaking at a higher-than-natural pitch might make you come off as less serious, or how using only your nickname might lead to people underestimating your authority. It's so easy to underestimate the impact of even the smallest behavioural cues.

Visual cues to inspire your inner yay

You might discover that your confidence-boosting prompts come not so much from physical activities but from tweaks to your environment. I personally find visual cues and affirmations to be extremely helpful for guiding my thinking in the right direction. I have always been a great lover of plastering impactful motivational quotes around my home and desk as a sort of safety net to spark positive thinking in case I lose track throughout the day. You might already know that I've even gone so far as to publish a *Seize the Yay* flip book filled with motivational quotes and positive affirmations to perch wherever you need them most (because there are only so many Post-it notes you can go through).

In her book *Happy, Healthy, Strong*, the delightful Rachael Finch describes how she uses positive affirmations before going on camera or in other vulnerable situations to bring back the confidence and positivity she needs. She describes self-belief and confidence so beautifully as being like building a house: it takes dedicated time and effort, and involves lots of different elements, which help contribute to making it an overall home and keeping you safe. If you're not into wall art, you might find other techniques or environmental factors like mood boards or a playlist uplifting and reassuring. Whatever cues make you feel stronger and more resilient in the face of self-doubt, embrace them as wholly as you can and as often as you need.

Strategy 2: Journal through the fears

In some scenarios, it makes sense to dash to the bathroom and whip out a two-minute power pose before you head into a meeting or jump on stage. In other situations, a quieter, gentler approach might be more suitable, particularly outside the context of real-time events or moments in time, such as the longer-term endeavour of starting a business. Many of us are aware of how important it is to carefully consider how we speak to others around us, but too often we forget to monitor how we speak to ourselves – after all, you might actually be listening. Self-dialogue can be another incredibly important tool in quelling the destructive whispers of impostor syndrome, and one of my favourite ways to do this is with a journal.

Like the power pose, journalling was a strategy I only discovered a few years after starting Matcha Maiden (although that never stopped me accumulating piles of beautiful journals to save for a rainy day). While it would have been great to have had the clarity and focus a good writing session can provide in the early days of our business, I've wasted no time catching up since then and now lean heavily on my journal not only in business but also as a tool for managing my mental health.

Journalling is a well-recognised, fantastic and powerful tool for any kind of self-work, but it's particularly good for boosting self-confidence. While it might seem a little odd to sit in front of a mirror and have a full-blown con-versation with yourself out loud (although each to their own, I wouldn't begrudge you if that worked well for you), turning to a journal to download and help reorientate all your thoughts or talk yourself around to a positive mindset is probably an easier and somewhat less awkward option for most of us.

 Self-dialogue can be another incredibly important tool in quelling the destructive whispers of impostor syndrome.

A great proponent of the power of journalling, unsurprisingly, is Kristina Karlsson, founder of Swedish stationery brand Kikki.K. I've had the pleasure of spending time with Kristina on several occasions, including one of my very first podcast episodes, and I've heard her speak about how putting pen to paper at 3 am one night led her to the idea for Kikki.K. Kristina grew up on a small farm in rural Sweden but moved to Australia in her early twenties with her partner, Paul. They were living pay cheque to pay cheque at the time and she was overwhelmed with adjusting to a new country, language and culture. She also had no idea what she wanted to do with her life. In the middle of the night, she was awoken several times by this disorienting question, so Paul suggested she write down some of the things that were important to her as a starting point – to help her get some direction.

Kristina now refers to this as her '3 am list', and views the process of writing all her hopes and dreams down, and casting aside all limiting thoughts and beliefs as a profoundly pivotal moment in her life. With no university degree, training, experience or money to start the business, Kristina grew the dreams on her 3 am list into a global stationery empire with over 100 stores all over the world and 250+ stockists covering 147+ countries. Like many international retail businesses, Kristina's business has had its share of challenges and ups and downs, and through the toughest of times she credits her daily journalling with keeping her balanced, positive and focused. Her daily morning routine includes three pages of conscious writing, pouring out everything she is thinking and feeling. She says this helps her explore how fears or risks might be keeping her stuck, as well as helping her work through ways to move forward. Her book, *Your Dream Life Starts Here*, includes a section called 'The Power of Putting Pen to Paper', and a companion Kikki.K *Dream Life Journal* with worksheets and journalling space accompanies the corresponding chapters of the book.

For some of you, a similar approach to Kristina's might help you get some distance and perspective from feelings of self-doubt, and help you observe and sort through them rather than being swept up completely. Writing things down helps us see them from a new, more objective perspective than when they're left bubbling around unchallenged in your head. For me, this has been useful not only when dissecting feelings of self-doubt, but also during crippling bouts of disorienting anxiety. Sometimes, what might seem hugely scary or overwhelming in your mind is nowhere near as scary once you've made it real by writing it down on paper and confronting it head-on.

By journalling and exploring how we honestly feel in a safe space, away from what others might think about what we're saying, we can face up to those fears and evaluate them with more clarity. In the case of self-doubt, this process often helps us realise that those fears are irrational and over-exaggerated. As in Kristina's case, this then makes it easier to start identifying areas we are getting stuck, as well as turning our minds to possible ways to move through them. Sometimes, the process itself is cathartic too; getting doubtful, unhelpful feelings all out of your system and onto paper helps you acknowledge and then move past them.

Focus on the yays, not the nays

If journalling about your fears and doubts doesn't appeal to you, then you may benefit from writing down the things you *are* confident about. For some, the benefit might come from writing down your goals and the things that you are confident about in order to get closer to them. You might not be so easily able to remember your strengths and all the reasons you are, in fact, equipped for what you're about to embark on in your mind – where things undoubtedly get messy and carried away – but writing them down can help you stay focused on them. It can be a great way of realising that your doubts make up a much smaller piece of the pie than you initially believed.

I'm sure I'm not alone in having spent far too much time criticising myself and identifying areas I wanted to improve in while spending very little time turning the tables and committing to writing down the things I'd done well or was good at. If I had spent a little more time on this kind of affirming journalling *before* we started Matcha Maiden, I would have been able to see that my existing skill set and strengths, as well as Nic's, were actually quite relevant to the process of getting a business off the ground. I would have seen that we weren't nearly as unqualified or unprepared as we thought we were, even if we weren't *directly* qualified or experienced. Highlighting your skills and abilities in this concrete way, rather than focusing repeatedly on areas you're lacking, can give you a huge confidence boost and reassurance when you need it most.

There is, in fact, scientific data on the benefit of committing your goals to writing and positively visualising them coming to life. A goal-setting study by Gail Matthews PhD from the Dominican University of California found that people were up to 42 per cent more likely to achieve their goals if they wrote them down – that's huge! From a practical viewpoint, goal-oriented journalling encourages you to whittle down the lofty, vague expressions of the goals swimming around in your mind into a clearly defined, properly articulated written expression. From a scientific viewpoint, this process increases the chances of you pushing through the disruptive feelings of self-doubt and fear to make that goal happen.

Writing down a goal and, even better, creating a process map or 'mind map' of how you're going to achieve it or visualising its implementation, encourages and guides your brain into cooperating with the plan. It also introduces elements of tangibility, measurability and accountability into the exercise, which you don't have when your goals are left unexpressed. Writing down your vision makes it easier to set out the concrete steps you need to take next, and harder to walk away from when you're feeling uncertain or unmotivated. There is a permanence or seriousness to seeing your goals on paper that doesn't apply the same way to ideas that you haven't yet articulated outside your own thinking space.

Some people might say that there are better ways to journal than others, but there's no universally accepted technique for this process of downloading things from your mind. You might find that it's not so much the individual entries that are helpful to you but rather the comparison between several – showing how far you've come in a certain time, proving your self-growth and giving you milestones to celebrate. You might find that journalling simply helps relieve the stress and tension caused by bottling up feelings you feel you can't express elsewhere. After all, it's harder to stay positive and motivated when you're stressed out and emotionally or physically exhausted.

Like everything on your way to yay, the strategies that work for you will be deeply personal and involve a bit of trial and error. I have experimented with lots of different lengths, durations, pens, pages, line distance, colours and everything else you could think of to work out exactly what helps my mind-mapping process the most. Journalling might make your impostor syndrome worse or it might not do much at all, but it could also lead to a breakthrough and become a vital tool in your confidence toolbox. Next time you're having trouble orientating your thoughts or feelings, try putting pen to paper and seeing what happens.

Workshop your worst-case scenario

This strategy is very personal and anecdotal, but it's one I find most useful when facing self-doubt, and that's to talk a situation through to its worst-case scenario. A big component of self-doubt or impostor syndrome is fear: fear of failure, fear of looking silly, fear of rejection by others. Confronting that fear head-on strips it of its power. Whether it be something you write about in your journal or something you discuss physically with a trusted friend or family member, I find that actually talking about or writing down the things that could go wrong makes them far less intimidating and overwhelming. I feel the same way about horror movies; the build-up of suspense and terror is all-consuming until you catch a glimpse of the monster. Then you can process what it is only to realise it's not nearly as bad as you thought when you let your mind get carried away.

This approach doesn't necessarily work in cases where the risks involved *are* quite substantial, so I don't recommend it if you're embarking on something that involves a huge financial investment or a similarly sizeable risk, as it will only highlight that there *is* a lot at stake and that things *could* go quite badly. In those cases, I suggest seeking the assistance of a professional who can run you through those scenarios with an experienced and realistic eye. That said, in many cases, the worst possible outcome isn't nearly as terrible as we think and this process helps me reflect on whether my self-doubt is rational, and based on real risk, or simply a protective mechanism that pops up when I do something new or outside the comfort zone. Usually I end up convinced that there's nothing to rationally fear at all and that nothing awful or life-shattering is going to result from my decision, even if things don't go well.

In other cases, this process can highlight areas for me where I can actually act to reduce the possibility of things going badly. Potential problems I might not have otherwise considered come up when doing this and being able to troubleshoot this way instils more confidence in me that now we are equipped for things to work out as we plan. For me, this exercise constitutes a big part of my journalling when working on my confidence levels. If I'm feeling stuck, or crippled by worry or lack of self-belief, I will sit down for a few hours and really investigate what my fear is based on and try to dissect it to make it less overwhelming.

It can provide you with the perspective you need to put your impostor syndrome in context and see it as an emotional reflex rather than the truth about your abilities. If the worst-case scenario isn't really that terrible, then everything that goes according to plan (or better) counts as a fabulous bonus. You can even flip the conversation into what I've heard referred to as 'reverse paranoia', which is when you start focusing on all the reasons why you *could* end up with your best-case scenario. Again, it's just a mental exercise of putting things in a 'yay-frame' in a way that's helpful rather than destructive. I continue to be reminded about how happiness is much less about how things *are* and much more about how we *see* them.

In the case of Matcha Maiden, as we were going to be stuck with the stock we'd purchased either way, there wasn't ultimately going to be a financial impact if we failed to sell any product at all. The net result of putting Matcha Maiden out there was that not a single tangible thing would change, unless it were a positive change and, hence, a bonus. When Nic and I workshopped Matcha Maiden together, the only potential negative result we could identify is that we might feel a little silly having put ourselves out there with this grand business idea that didn't ever work. We look silly most of the time anyway, so that was no biggie at all.

 I continue to be reminded about how happiness is much less about how things *are* and much more about how we *see* them.

In general, I think many of us grossly overestimate the amount of attention others are paying to the finer details of our lives. Even if we do look silly to a few people for a few moments in time, is that really such a big deal in the grand scheme of things? If a small dent to our pride was the very worst that could happen, we weren't risking much at all, and any small success we had in selling even one bag would be a wonderful bonus, let alone if the business eventually took off and did well. Once we put that into perspective, suddenly the whole thing didn't seem so scary, risky or impossible, and a rush of confidence came back in.

Of course, six months later, after our fledgling business took off we had to talk through a new worst-case scenario as I weighed up whether to walk away from a stable income and steady career to take a financial risk on a business idea that had no guarantee of growing big enough to replace my wage. By that time, however, we had given the business (and ourselves) some time to at least prove it could generate *some* profits and grow to a point where it wasn't as financially scary to make the jump. This time, if things didn't work out and the business was a flop, we'd be down the cash that we had already spent (no small sum, but also not a devastating loss in the grand scheme of life) and I'd have to go back to a job as a lawyer. By this point in my legal career, I'd established a good reputation and some great relationships, and I knew I could either apply to the same firm again or find work at a similar one. It was no longer mid-GFC, and I was past the entry-level graduate stage where thousands of candidates were vying for very limited positions. So, again, the biggest risk we faced was a small dent in our pride and a few months of our lives.

I have come back to this strategy of talking things through over and over. Since becoming better at managing impostor syndrome, I've become a serial starter of new things. When launching our café and my podcast saw me return to the throes of doubting myself, I turned again to this strategy to help me get a realistic grip on my creeping doubts that I was unworthy and unlikely to be able to pull it off. As with Matcha Maiden, I had no technical experience in hospitality or in podcasting, so journalling to write down all the relevant skills I had was not going to be helpful or confidence-boosting in these particular situations. What *was* helpful, however, was meaningfully exploring the worst-case scenarios and realising they wouldn't signal the end of the world.

From a nuts and bolts perspective, Matcha Mylkbar was intended as more of a pop-up eatery to begin with, so, along with our business partners, Nic and I did most of the physical fit-out ourselves and we only needed a modest investment to get it off the ground. Similarly, the *Seize the Yay* podcast was relatively low stakes: it began as a non-monetary creative hobby to legitimise my desire to chat for hours with interesting people, and the only investment required was the purchase of some entry-level equipment that could be easily on-sold if I chose not to continue with it. Allowing myself to explore all the possible outcomes of these projects helped me to get a true measure of the worst-possible situation and weigh it up against the best-possible outcome to make informed decisions accordingly. Rather than acting on the impostor syndrome and deciding against beginning at all, talking down the risks and playing up the potential benefits of giving these projects a go helped allay my fears and bolster my confidence levels.

Flipping things on their head and further pushing that into a 'reverse paranoia' exercise also encouraged me to focus my energy and attention on the practical things I could do to increase the chances of success, such as consulting with mentors or upskilling in certain areas, rather than getting bogged down or paralysed by self-doubt and doing nothing at all. A highly effective way to arm yourself against doubting your abilities is to do whatever you can to practically improve them. Self-doubt makes it very difficult to get perspective on these kinds of priorities in the moment. But if you can learn how to acknowledge it then push it aside, you can focus on what you need to do to get closer to your best-case scenario.

Strategy 3: (Neuro)plastic surgery and underthinking

When it comes to mindset, someone I have learned so much from is Shelley Laslett. She's a neuroscience coach, CEO and co-founder of Vitae, a start-up adviser, strategist, social scientist and many other things. Shelley and I met, of all places, in sunny Fiji when we were speakers at the Nurture Her immersive business retreat (another example of a place I could never have dreamed I'd get to work in). I was blown away by her keynote speech on the neuroscience of leadership.

We stayed in touch afterwards, and I was lucky enough to have her as a guest on my podcast. We spent an hour diving deeper into the topic of rewiring neural pathways to improve confidence, performance and happiness, and the discussion blew my mind. Her version of upskilling to keep self-doubt and worst-case scenarios at bay involves completing a masters of neuroscience to add to her other qualifications. But even at her level, she brushes this off as knowing nothing compared to the 'real scientists'.

Shelley refers to the above forms of self-dialogue and self-investigation as presenting the opportunity to perform '(neuro)plastic surgery' on ourselves and rewire unhelpful thoughts and perceptions. She describes her coaching work as helping others get from where they are to where they want to be, but she reminds her clients that *they* are their own brain surgeons with the control and metaphorical scalpel in their hands. What patterns of thinking can we cut and hack? What processes and negative thoughts or stories we've been telling ourselves can we completely scrap from our thinking? After all, nothing and nobody can make us feel anything internally without us first giving it or them our permission. And, luckily, we have a 'braking system' thanks to our prefontal cortex to change the way we respond to those factors.

The crux of the techniques that Shelley teaches is that we need to be able to think about our own thoughts and reflect on them. She taught me the term for this: meta-cognition. Metacognition is generally separated into two different steps: firstly, thinking about our thoughts (e.g. *I am experiencing self-doubt*). Secondly, regulating those thoughts or cognitive processes (e.g. *This is an unproductive thought that I won't let go any further*).

Again, without getting too science-y, one of the most exciting emerging areas of brain research is that of neuroplasticity. Basically, our brains are like plastic and our brain cells which form connections, called synapses, create pathways and these continuously change throughout our lives. These connections can reorganise themselves in response to new situations or changes in our environment. Through thinking differently, you can actually train your brain to weaken negative pathways and create new and preferred ones at any time. It's worth some further research if you're interested in that kind of thing.

The good news is that you're not stuck with the ways of thinking that you're born with. In fact, you can rewire the thought patterns that aren't serving you at any time in your life. Next time you feel completely stuck or disadvantaged by old, crippling ways of thinking, remember that you are completely able to rewire these negative pathways and leave self-doubt behind. As I've mentioned, the goal is not to *never* feel self-doubt or inadequacy again – overconfidence comes with its own set of problems – but rather to know how to respond to them swiftly and effectively when they do pop by to say hello. Once you understand your thought processes as something you can mould to your benefit, you have so much more capacity for achieving your greatest potential.

In terms of how you *actually* change a neural pathway, there are many technical scientific examples of neuroplasticity, like the adult brain recovering after a stroke. For our purposes though, there are simpler day-to-day practices that can help reshape your thought patterns that I've found extremely useful in managing self-doubt, catastrophising and even anxiety. Two widely accepted ways to rewire the brain's emotional responses are through mindful meditation and cognitive behavioural therapy, both of which I practise regularly, both independently as well as with a therapist. But even just practising awareness and metacognition to break habitual thought patterns – acknowledging the thought, evaluating whether it's helpful or harmful and deciding how you want to respond – rather than surrendering to those thoughts can prevent you from spiralling into despair and fear of failure.

 Once you understand your thought processes as something you can mould to your benefit, you have so much more capacity for achieving your greatest potential.

For example, a concern that plagued me at the beginning of Matcha Maiden was my lack of qualifications or training for the business journey we were embarking upon, and how dire the consequences of that could be. When those doubts returned as we prepared to launch Matcha Mylkbar, I had the skill set to interrupt those fears as soon as they arrived, and counter them. I reminded myself that I hadn't needed those qualifications to grow Matcha Maiden into a success and learning on the go had served us just fine. Years later, when it came to starting the podcast, my lack of two clues to rub together about audio editing or production barely registered as a blip on the radar (or at least not a big one). I felt the doubts enter and exit my brain barely minutes apart because I had trained myself to acknowledge, then push unhelpful feelings away – and this technique had done wonders for my confidence. Like anything, you get better with practise, so get into that neuroplastic surgery and watch yourself thrive!

Less thinking, more doing

While it is common, perhaps even inevitable, to spend a lot of time thinking and overthinking things before getting started on a new idea or project, there is something to be said for not only cutting out negative thought patterns or thinking *through* them, but rather skipping them altogether.

In fact, this can be a winning strategy in itself to combat the dangers of the impostor syndrome: make a speedy decision and course-correct as you go.

As I mentioned earlier, naivety can actually work in your favour when you first start something new; if you don't know too much about what lies ahead, there's less that can scare you away. The founder and global CEO of Business Chicks, Emma Isaacs (one of my greatest role models and friends), wrote a whole book, called *Winging It*, about the powerful tool that underthinking can be, especially for helpless overthinkers like myself.

As Emma mentions in relation to her personal life, let alone her business journey, some of the best decisions of her life are the fastest ones she's made. She moved in with her husband, Rowan, after dating for less than a month, they were engaged after six months, married the next year and she was pregnant with their first child three months after that. Emma also bought her company, Business Chicks, on the spot at the very same event where it was announced that the (then-fledgling) networking group was going to close unless someone was interested in taking it over. Rather than give any creeping feelings of self-doubt airtime, or overthink something she knew had incredible potential, she listened to the persistent voice in her head saying, *You'd be mad not to do this*, and went ahead anyway.

In her book, she explains, 'If I think about the times when I've taken too long to make decisions on things I've really wanted to do, the main reason was fear. Fear of not having enough money. Fear that I was not good enough. Fear that I'd fail. When I finally pushed through the fear and committed to the choice I knew deep down I wanted to make, none of these things proved true.' Since then, Emma has grown Business Chicks into a hugely successful global movement uniting women around the world and creating the largest and most influential network for women in Australia. This organisation has connected thousands of women, raised over $12 million for charity and brought some of the world's best and brightest minds to Australia including Brené Brown, Gloria Steinem, Elizabeth Gilbert, Jamie Oliver, Arianna Huffington, Seth Godin, Sophia Amoruso and Nigella Lawson.

One of the incredible events on the jam-packed Business Chicks schedule is an annual retreat to Necker Island, Sir Richard Branson's private island in the Caribbean – such is the influence and network Emma has been able to build. I was flabbergasted but thrilled to be invited to join the 2019 cohort. A week before our wedding, I spent a transformative, perspective-shifting, life-changing seven days with 20 other women and Sir Richard. Stories of the bachelorette party they threw me will come in detail later.

Among the many highlights for me was hearing Laura Brown, the inimitable editor-in-chief of *InStyle* magazine, speak to us about her journey. Her own way to yay into Manhattan's elite began humbly on a New South Wales dairy farm. Laura is, among many other things, another huge proponent of the art of underthinking. In an article for *Thrive Global*, she says 'Overthinking, to me, is fatal. It is an express pass to self-doubt. Have you ever heard anyone say, "I overthought it, and it came out great!" You haven't, because it doesn't.' She echoed these thoughts when we chatted for my podcast, and truer words were never spoken.

Having started out as a lawyer, overthinking has been one of the hardest patterns for me to break since becoming an entrepreneur. All of my training focused on attention to detail, covering absolutely all bases, and leaving no stone unturned when it came to things that could go wrong down the track. That made it incredibly hard to get things done when I first realised how fast-paced and agile small businesses need to be and held up many crucial decisions in the expansion of Matcha Maiden. But I have gradually learned to flip the underthinking switch and act before I have time to delve into all the possible scenarios.

I'm a personality of great extremes: I'm either overthinking or not thinking at all. This gradual transition has absolutely confirmed Laura's declaration that overthinking never made anything better. Yes, you absolutely should do *some* thinking about what you're about to embark on, but only enough that you can start. The rest can be fixed and updated as you go.

Another thing I noticed very early on about myself when it came to overthinking – something I suspect many of you may share – was a persistent need to 'poll' decisions before I'd make them. If I felt particularly struck down by self-doubt, my default move was to ask as many people around me what they thought in order to break my internal deadlock. Coming back to *Nice Girls Don't Get the Corner Office*, a major theme of Dr Frankel's book is that the people around you and the impact they have on your mindset is crucial, but not to the extent that it should prevent you from making clear and timely decisions. Another great learning I took away from her book was the difference between 'participative decision making' and the inability to act without knowing what everyone else thinks and whether they approve. You don't want to let the pendulum swing too far in the opposite direction and live the lone wolf life to the exclusion of valuable input and advice. However, part of underthinking involves being able to move forward without a full questionnaire being submitted to your trusted sources.

If I felt particularly struck down by self-doubt, my default move was to ask as many people around me what they thought in order to break my internal deadlock.

If you dare venture a step further down the under-thinking, spontaneous decision-making pathway, someone who always brings me right back down to earth when I've been swept away by the self-doubt fairies is Mark Manson. You've likely heard of his *New York Times* best-selling book, *The Subtle Art of Not Giving a F*ck* – not to be confused with Sarah Knight's best-selling and equally impactful *The Life-Changing Magic of Not Giving a F**k*. (Clearly, we're onto something here.) Manson's book can lighten even the dreariest of impostor-syndrome-infested moods thanks to his blunt, profanity-filled reminders that life's too short to agonise and overthink everything. It has a lot of F-bombs, but his point is clear: there is a very subtle and vitally important art in learning how to focus and prioritise your thoughts effectively. Sometimes, you have to be able to care less about the things that will hold you back from your ultimate yay. It's all about nailing the perfect fuck distribution.

Manson describes how most of us will know someone who, at one time or another, gave no fucks and then went on to accomplish major things in their life. These, as he calls them, 'moments of non-fuckery' are the moments that most define our lives – they are the spontaneous switches in careers or starting brand-new businesses. Manson distinguishes underthinking from indifference or apathy; for him, it's about choosing not to get bogged down in feelings or emotions that don't serve you. With every interaction in life we are choosing, and we are responsible for the consequences of those choices. So, he's another great proponent for less thinking, more ripping of the bandaid and doing the big, scary thing. And while, of course, I don't mean that you should go completely rogue and not think at *all*, there is clearly something to be said for just getting things done, which leads beautifully into our next chapter on the art of just getting started.

CHAPTER 3

Done is better than perfect

Hand-in-hand with self-doubt and feelings of inadequacy comes our troublesome old mate, perfectionism. Perfection-ism is the definitional opposite of ripping off the bandaid or underthinking, and it stops as many ideas from getting off the ground as the dreaded impostor syndrome.

Having power posed and journalled myself to the point of believing Matcha Maiden was, in fact, a pretty solid idea that could surpass my initial expectations of failure, the next big hurdle I faced was the painstaking process of perfecting the idea for a potential launch. On the A-type to yay-type spectrum, this was well and truly early days for me, and my frantic colour-coding, Post-it-noting, to-do list making and excel spreadsheeting began.

At this point, the stark differences between Nic's work habits and mine (nay, our whole personalities) came into clearer focus than ever before. Nic was naturally inclined towards spontaneity and Emma Isaac's 'winging it' model of getting shit done. In contrast, my legally trained, bullet point-loving side was still dominating my psyche, and becoming increasingly honed with each year I spent in a corporate legal office. While these detail-oriented traits of mine were wonderful for the initial set-up of our business, as we sorted out a corporate structure, trademarked the business name and dealt with other administrative stuff, it proved seriously obstructive to anything beyond that (except perhaps at tax time).

While attention to detail is no doubt an excellent quality to have (and one I'm still grateful to my legal training for), *obsession* with detail is particularly unhelpful in the dynamic and fast-paced world of start-ups. Left to my own devices, I would have spent months, if not years, tackling branding details such as consistent font sizing and checking we were using a long dash rather than a short one uniformly across all materials. I would have agonised over things that, ultimately, as it turns out, didn't matter at all or ended up changing very quickly after the launch and I don't think we ever would have launched at all. I'm forever grateful to Nic for his mind-opening influence on me and his insistence on my now treasured motto, that 'done is better than perfect'.

 Obsession with detail is particularly unhelpful in the dynamic and fast-paced world of start-ups.

With Nic's gentle but persistent encouragement, I eventually started to relax into the idea that a 75 per cent finished product that we could launch had far more chance of success than a product we took so long perfecting that we never launched at all. Of course, particularly in the case of consumable goods like matcha powder, there are bare minimum food safety and nutritional labelling guidelines that do have to be 100 per cent right (for good reason), so I'm not encouraging you to scrap your planning or refining. What I am encouraging you to do is remember that all you really need to launch is a minimum viable product or service. There are two main reasons I always come back to for moving on something before it's perfect:

1. Our fast-paced world imposes time pressures on many ideas or life changes. Sit on something for too long waiting for the 'perfect moment', and you might miss the moment altogether. How awful would it be to have a wonderful idea for ages and then see someone else execute it first?

2. Even if you do continue to refine over and over until you genuinely believe you've moulded it into the perfect product or idea, what *you* think is perfect might not be what your target audience thinks is perfect, or what works perfectly in practice, meaning you're likely to have to make changes anyway.

So, apart from the legals and regulatory non-negotiables, Nic's method won and we got our business to market in three short weeks from that first humble serviette scribble to a fully operational online store. For us, 'done' was far less sophisticated than you would ever imagine – many new beginnings are, despite what the polished, end-product might have you to believe. With our makeshift production line and homemade website, we ran a very ad-hoc DIY operation to begin with, just enough to get the business off the ground. We did what we could with what we had between us, and barely spent more than the cash we'd outlaid for the matcha to get us to that minimum viable product.

I always come back to our very early days and think about how well that very basic, initial set-up served us to remind me that, in most cases, you really *can* get started on a business, project or dream with much less fuss, cash and overthinking than you might expect. Again, the glorification of busy can creep in here, leading you to plan forever and *feel* productive instead of actually starting. Over the past few years, these reflections have led me to add a second prong to the done-is-better-than-perfect motto. It may sound a little contradictory and even anti-yay at face value, but I've found this enormously helpful through our journey. Allow me to introduce you to my 'Dream big, plan small' approach. Dream big enough to excite you to start, but small enough so you actually can.

Dream big, plan small

Dreaming big is all the rage, for good reason. Another saying I love in the 'dream big' vein is that unless your dreams scare you a little bit, you're probably not aiming high enough. What this doesn't address, though, is that those dreams might be so big that they scare you off starting at all. So while I am absolutely a huge fan of dreaming big and thinking as far beyond your current reality and limits as you can when it comes to *conceiving* of your idea, I also believe it's important to scale that back to smaller, more realistic steps when *implementing* it. I've come to realise that all things in life are just a mind game, and if you can master your mind, your external circumstances matter less and less – the big trick is knowing how and when to direct your thinking one way or the other. So, when I'm *dreaming* I make a concerted effort to think/talk things up as much as I can, but when I'm *doing*, I talk them all the way back down.

The problem with thinking on a macro level is over-whelm – the enormity of bringing everything to life at once and as a whole. By breaking things down to much smaller increments and tackling them one at a time, things become much less intimidating and infinitely more achievable. When we started Matcha Maiden we didn't try to create the business it is today all in one go; we never would have started or succeeded if we'd tried to. Instead, the main goal we set was simply to sell one single bag of matcha powder to a stranger who wasn't already in our network.

Framing things that way stopped us wasting too much time worrying about things that weren't yet relevant and might never have become relevant. Our small goal made it seem manageable enough to achieve. We had certainly dreamed that the idea could then take off and grow (not to where it has, but certainly further than one bag) but planned small and focused only on the *immediate* next step necessary to put things into motion. After all, the reality of life is that you can physically only be in one place taking one step at a time anyway (even if there is a bit of multi-tasking within that step), so why look too much further ahead and get caught up in its magnitude?

A few years later, I came back to this dream big, plan small approach when starting the *Seize the Yay* podcast. Though the podcast started in late 2018, I actually had registered the business name early in 2017 (see, my legal background still comes in handy). Similar to Matcha Maiden, it simply struck me one day that this phrase was the perfect way to describe my newly developed philosophy on life. Even though I wasn't sure what format it would take, I went ahead and registered the name anyway.

By late 2018, I had developed huge dreams for my new Seize the Yay brand. I envisioned it being an overarching yay-making community with lots of different offshoots to help people shape an exciting, fulfilling life. This community would include things like an event series, an online channel and merchandise – I still hope it will. However, if I'd set out to build something that complex and broad straight off the bat, I would have been too overwhelmed by the enormity of getting it off the ground, especially with running our other two businesses.

Instead, I chose to start with a narrower, far less intimidating focus. Launching a podcast was more finite and approachable than the all-encompassing brand. Even then, though, if I'd thought of it becoming the podcast it is today, with millions of downloads and a line-up of guests I'm in awe of, I probably wouldn't have started. Like we'd done with Matcha Maiden, I focused only on the next, immediate step. The first was figuring out how to record, edit and publish a single, audible episode to my initial listener(s). The rest was future Sarah's problem.

I came back to my trusty 'done is better than perfect' approach to begin and opted for an act of commitment (like that initial purchase of matcha powder) that would force me into making it happen. Within two weeks of having the idea to start the podcast, I enlisted Nic's help with the technical research and we bought the recording equipment and software that I still use over a year later. To give myself a hard deadline, I also approached the first guest I wanted to interview, *Shark Tank* investor and *Survivor* contestant Janine Allis, founder of Boost Juice and parent company, Retail Zoo. We were scheduled to speak at the same conference in Fiji a few weeks later so if we were going to record over there, I had to get myself into gear very quickly.

In the end, I didn't end up recording with Janine until much later, and Rachael Finch became my first interviewee, but having that deadline had forced me to figure out where the bloody hell podcasts live and how to make one. Again, I'd jumped in headfirst to a new venture, with no knowledge or experience of podcasts or audio editing and production.

But, as you now know, Google is one of my dearest friends; it can be the best of mentors in almost any endeavour you could imagine, so gradually, with Google as my ally, I was able to work out how to do one episode without too much trouble, and the rest followed from there. It's true that I still find myself apologising to people who are qualified in these areas for not doing things the 'proper way', but even so I haven't looked back.

At one point, I did start to worry a little that this 'planning small' approach was anti-yay in that it necessitated me to somewhat talk down my dreams, and I reverted to some serious overthinking until I realised I'm not the only one who adopts this philosophy. Cyan Ta'eed, who launched the online creative marketplace Envato with her husband, Collis, from her parents' garage, has also been a wonderful podcast guest of mine – she has reassured me that she overthinks, too. When I talked to her, she told me how she'd been working as a freelance graphic designer and was dissatisfied with the huge percentage that creative marketplaces were taking from creatives for stock assets sold on those platforms. They started Envato to provide an alternative platform for creatives, and focused on lowering their cut per sale as they grew. Now, Envato sellers take up to 80 per cent of the proceeds from a sale as opposed to the 10 per cent Cyan once made. Since starting Envato,

Cyan has started a hand-made chocolate social enterprise called Hey Tiger, and launched the website-building app, Milkshake.

When she talked to me about starting small, Cyan said, 'What I found works for me over time is to really broadly visualise what [my dream] could look like and what fun it could be . . . but right now all we're trying to do is get from here to here.' Throughout her career, Cyan explains that she has simply followed what she's been interested in; she's considered each new venture as an act of making or creating as opposed to starting a business. Importantly, she says that this 'dream big, plan small' way of thinking has freed her up a lot, explaining that there are certain ways of thinking that can be intimidating or unhelpful to you when you're getting started. Nic actually joined Envato as a customer in its very first year, and I've never seen him fangirl anybody before this interview.

Don't be fooled by Envato's humble beginnings, though – this mentality has clearly worked well for Cyan in growing her businesses to great success. Envato has grown to over 650 employees and earned creatives over USD$900 million since 2006, dramatically changing the landscape in her industry. Cyan personally has become one of Australia's richest women through the business' rapid expansion. And her Hey Tiger chocolate is on its own exciting growth trajectory – it's THE most delicious and innovative chocolate, and it also supports community development projects in West Africa.

Despite this amazing success story, my inner lawyer feels the need to pop a disclaimer in here (even though the following probably doesn't need to be spelled out): by encouraging you to plan small and focus on each next step as it presents itself, I don't mean that you should ignore or fail to prepare for any further steps you need to take. I just mean you shouldn't get so carried away with planning those future steps that they interfere with your focus on the vital step you should be dealing with right now. An age-old adage attributed to many thought leaders, particularly Benjamin Franklin, that absolutely rings true here is, 'Fail to plan and you plan to fail'. It is, of course, important to have considered all the steps you might need to take and have some idea of what they might look like, even if they are way down the track or unlikely.

Admittedly, Nic and I never had an official business plan, but after the first business hurdles we encountered (like running out of our product immediately), we did start to think at least a few bags of matcha ahead – about what might be needed at the next stage of growth. It was great to briefly consider that we might eventually ship globally or expand into other products one day, even if we didn't invest time in that kind of research or infrastructure at the expense of simply fulfilling the orders we had and keeping things afloat. We didn't need to prioritise preparing for those things at the beginning stages, especially given our time and funding for this side hustle was limited to begin with. It all comes back to a minimum viable product and taking the immediate next steps required to bring that to life. This is why you hear so many stories of businesses started for peanuts in parents' garages. You simply don't NEED to start at the end!

Conception of a virgin

An example of dreaming big and planning small that I loved discovering is that of Virgin Atlantic, the brainchild of the ultimate entrepreneur, Sir Richard Branson. He shared many wonderful stories during our time on Necker Island, and if I thought starting a matcha tea business online was overwhelming, I can't comprehend the mental gymnastics that would have been required to get a new airline off the ground, not least as an industry outsider. Think about it for more than a few minutes and you can see how easy it would be to crumble at the prospect of buying all the planes, hiring all the staff, getting all the licensing approvals and the million and one other things it takes to transport people across the world safely and efficiently. Even though he was already quite the businessman at the time, this seems impossibly daunting.

I was delighted to learn that the very first expression of Virgin Atlantic was Sir Richard's spontaneous response to being stuck on the tarmac trying to leave Puerto Rico for the British Virgin Islands. His flight was grounded, and he had already been away from his girlfriend (now-wife), Joan, for weeks, and was absolutely fed up. Right there and then, he decided to charter a private plane. He figured out how much it would cost if the expenses were pooled between other travellers, then popped the resulting sum up on a chalkboard advertising Virgin Atlantic's first flight. He was not so much dreaming big, planning small as much as not really pre-planning at all!

In one of his many insightful books, *Finding My Virginity*, Sir Richard says that many experts will tell you that it can take upwards of a year to get a business going, from the initial planning phase and market research to implementation and launch. He then goes on to say that he has always disregarded this rule and advises anyone following it to 'pull their finger out'. I was very reassured to read that the best ideas don't always need to be supported by detailed financial projections and extensive business plans (none of ours have involved anything similar). The third chapter of the book is appropriately titled, 'Building a Business from the Back of a Beer Mat'. In it, he describes how the plan for Virgin Australia started on the back of a beer mat and was fleshed out from there in just a day. This made us feel better about the Matcha Maiden serviette meeting.

Smaller beginnings can make for exceptionally wonderful outcomes because they allow you to just start and grow into things as you go. Aussie success story, Carolyn Creswell, started Carman's Kitchen by buying a tiny at-home muesli business for just A$1000 from a couple she worked for. She has since grown Carman's into a multi-million-dollar empire. Melanie Gleeson, founder of one of my favourite health havens, Endota Spa, started the now-national network of heavenly day spas with just one single venue in Mornington, Victoria, using A$5000 on a credit card and the help of her family. Endota Spa now employs close to 1000 people and about 90 per cent of those are women. There are countless people whose businesses have far surpassed their initial plans or ideas for them. By starting small, they've given their idea the time and energy needed to flourish.

Slow and steady

The other thing about dreaming big and planning small is that it not only helps you to conceptualise your first steps in terms of confidence, it also helps you logistically grow into your business or idea. I won't deny that there's a very fine line between an appropriate level of preparation and winging it, and this can be difficult to discern, but if you overprepare in the early days, striving for the 'perfect' set-up, you could sink your idea before it can grow its wings.

If we'd started off ordering the volumes of bags and labels we do now (even though the unit price is much cheaper) and using the packing facility we now use, our initial outlays would have been so big we wouldn't have had any money for anything else and wouldn't have gone much further. While it's been wonderful to be able to access better economies of scale as we've gotten bigger, and start to see better pricing and other conveniences appear, there's such a thing as scaling up too hard, too fast.

Taking things slower when it came to growing our business worked to our advantage in so many ways. Our initial goals were so conservative that we grew into each stage of business as we were ready, and this gave us time to review, consolidate and refine as we went along. We focused simply on what we needed to get done at that specific stage rather than pre-empting what would be perfect down the track. This meant asking ourselves what we needed to fulfil the orders we currently had without worrying too much about what the future of the business might require.

While it's been wonderful to be able to access better economies of scale as we've gotten bigger, and start to see better pricing and other conveniences appear, there's such a thing as scaling up too hard, too fast.

This slow and steady approach also allowed us to discover what our target market wanted. Even if you can afford extensive market research from the outset (which we definitely could not), you can never really predict how your target audience is going to react to your offering, or if they'll agree with what you perceive to be the ideal.

The concept of perfect has no meaning in a vacuum – only real-life feedback can guide you as to what will work and what won't. And the only way you can get that dialogue going is by biting the bullet and putting your idea out there for review. This is why the 'soft launch' has been increasingly popular; it allows you to test the real mechanisms of your business, but still with the opportunity for some tweaks and refinements before an official launch. And even if it turns out you have ticked most of the boxes early on, our modern society is changing constantly and, in some industries, every single day, so perfect isn't a static goalpost anyway.

Since that very first bag of matcha we sold, we have changed our bags, labels, logo, colours, website, tagline, packers, etc. – multiple times in some cases. One of the only things that hasn't changed is our tea farm. But we would never have arrived at the version of the product we're at now without going through each of those iterations and testing them against the scrutiny and demands of real customers. You can probably see the point I'm trying to make here, but in case your perfectionism is as stubborn as mine was and you need the point hammered home a little more, another beautiful quote that I find useful is this one from American author and motivational speaker, Hilary Hinton 'Zig' Ziglar: 'You don't have to be great to start, but you have to start to be great.'

The best part of getting started is that, in so many cases, you'll soon discover that you *were* in fact ready and/or great when you started, you just didn't *feel* that you were at the time. How many times have you heard an ultimately successful person looking back and saying, 'I was completely confident it would be exactly this successful'? And so, we come full circle, back to the previous chapter on the perils of self-doubt and how erroneous our self-(under)estimations often turn out to be. Perhaps Zig Ziglar's quote should be tweaked to, 'You don't have to *feel* great to start . . .' By starting, you give yourself the chance to find out whether you were or not and do something about it, rather than never knowing just how great you could be.

Fake it 'til you make it

We couldn't go much further into the territory of starting before you're ready without a nod to this terribly clichéd, but tried and tested approach to the early stages of any new venture. As much as this slogan is bandied around in jest, I have previously and continue to adopt it in all seriousness as a trusted strategy when feeling out of my depth and entering a new environment.

Turns out, much to my relief, many of my peers, role models and friends have also employed this approach on their own way to yay. There are, of course, contexts (such as in a book like this or most of the time in real life) where showing your vulnerability and uncertainty is important and valuable for your audience. In others, however – a job interview or a boardroom pitch – letting vulnerable feelings dominate might do you and your dreams a disservice. Even if, deep down, your inner peanut gallery is drowning in doubts and fears about what you're embarking on, there's something to be said for crafting a way of presenting yourself that gives you the confidence to start, and to be taken seriously, and holding onto it for dear life until your reality can catch up.

Of course, I don't mean that you should go faking your whole résumé and then stumble your way through life figuring out how to live up to it. (Although, full disclosure, I do know of more than one great success story that started that way and I definitely embellished a bit in my uni years.) For me, fake it 'til you make it is more of a gentle tool to combat the inevitable inner doubt while I'm in the 'total noob' stage of any activity. It allows me to press on long enough that I can become more competent and thereby confident.

It would be such a terrible shame to be talked out of the opportunity of a lifetime – and talked out of it *by your own mind*, for that matter – simply because it wasn't familiar or easily digested. Projecting confidence and affecting a mindset of optimism in the face of unfamiliarity sets up your internal environment to develop those feelings authentically in the long run. There is lots of scientific data on the power of body language and behaviours on your reality (again, I urge you to watch Amy Cuddy's TED talk). In any case, you're not pretending to be anyone else so much as helping yourself survive until you can realise who you already were.

A few months after launching Matcha Maiden, we started to see demand for our product from wholesalers and fully stepped into faking it 'til we made it (doesn't quite have the same ring in past tense). While we were unreservedly voicing our doubts and fears to each other and our loved ones in private, Nic and I presented as the picture of professionalism and confidence whenever we went out to pitch Matcha Maiden to new stockists, distributors or other potential partners.

Pitching is definitely one of those occasions where any internal hesitations or concerns for imperfection need not make an appearance. Thanks to Nic's agency, one area where we weren't completely unqualified was our creative infrastructure. Our website was highly sophisticated and immaculate, as were our 300 gsm business cards (if you aren't familiar, that's an impressively and unnecessarily thick cardstock). Our suite of marketing materials was perfectly coordinated – 'suite' belying the barely-two-person DIY operation we were running between full-time work in the dead of night.

From our prolific and polished social media, we gave the impression of an organised, corporate situation with a seamless, multi-person production line that was pushing drastic volumes and 'selling out' regularly as demand 'overwhelmed' us. And yet, if you only have two units of stock to begin with (an over-exaggeration but let's go with it), selling both of those units would be considered a 'sell-out', would it not?

Because matcha wasn't the ubiquitous ingredient it has now become, Nic and I also held a lot of tastings at the start mostly at yoga studios or other wellness hubs to attract new potential customers. I always have a giggle remembering how surprised people who knew of the business were to see me in an apron behind a table running the tastings myself, as if I had much more important 'CEO' things to be doing. Little did they know that the staff they probably assumed I was filling in for didn't exist and couldn't have been afforded in any case. I was the one running around the market, picking up ingredients, blending them myself and decanting them into jugs from the nearest two-dollar shop. I can't tell you how many times I've trawled thrift shops in cities all over the world to find appropriate jugs for this purpose before dashing to an event to set up a very professional-looking marketing stall with nobody any the wiser. Many loyal customers who have since heard the story of our beginnings have been astounded to line up their timelines and realise just how much of a newborn Matcha Maiden was when they first encountered it – believing it to be a large-scale operation from the beginning.

Behind the scenes, you could see how far we were from being the best candidates for the business we have ended up running today. Nic had a headstart on me as an entrepeneur, having run businesses before, but neither of us had prior experience in the world of manufacturing or importing.

We didn't even know what FMCG stood for (fast-moving consumer goods by the way. You're welcome!). You could say we didn't have a clue to share between us, but the 'winging it' method we spoke of earlier gave us a crash course in the majority of what we needed to know, while the faking it (mostly) melted away over time.

We never went so far as to outright deceive anyone as to our qualifications, instead, we adopted a more conservative 'underpromise and overdeliver' approach when it came to actual operations or commitments. It was that perception of competence that gained the attention of major retailers globally. Before long, we were stocked in retailers across the United States such as Urban Outfitters, and we'd locked in our national distributors in Australia – a relationship that continues today. This gave us the customer trust and momentum we needed to grow the business into the venture that our branding and (hopefully) flawless professional demeanours made it appear it already was.

Similarly, my relatively new Seize the Yay brand has only recently taken on enough of a life of its own to be called a 'business'. In our captions or emails I still almost always defer to 'we', 'us' and 'our', even though it's just little old me chugging along at this new side hustle while the matcha missions take up most of our time. Like I said, there's a fine line between faking it 'til you make it and outright deceiving people. But these small things help instil the confidence I need to bother continuing to the point where I *will* have a team behind me.

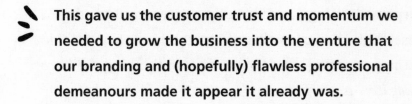

This gave us the customer trust and momentum we needed to grow the business into the venture that our branding and (hopefully) flawless professional demeanours made it appear it already was.

Be 100 per cent ready to figure things out

In my corporate lawyer life, this same fake it 'til you make it approach applied too, and I slowly learned that sometimes you just have to put yourself forward for something, even if you don't necessarily feel 100 per cent ready. Many times when I did this, I probably wouldn't have ever felt 100 per cent ready anyway.

As I mentioned earlier, one of the books I turned to regularly in the early years of my professional life in law was *Lean In* by Sheryl Sandberg, chief operating officer at Facebook. In her book, Sheryl discusses confidence and applying for corporate promotions using a fascinating Hewlett-Packard internal study. The findings of this struck me quite bluntly; so much so they have stayed with me since then – the study found that women would only apply for advertised jobs if they met 100 per cent of the criteria listed, whereas men would apply if they felt they met 60 per cent of the criteria. Sheryl points out, quite rightly, that this has a huge ripple effect on women's representation in corporate settings, and says that women need to adopt a mindset shift that takes them from thinking they can't do something to seeing what they want, and thinking, *I'll learn by doing it.*

Leaving gender aside, this lesson is invaluable: sometimes you *do* have to bite the bullet and learn as you go, lest you lose the opportunity to others who may act first. Nic and I might have only been 60 per cent ready (or less) in a practical sense to start Matcha Maiden and build it to thrive, but if we had waited until we felt closer to 100 per cent, we could have missed the opportunity to be first to market and *test* that market for real-time feedback to improve. It all comes back to having the confidence to start. Seeing someone else jump in to fill the gap first would have probably discouraged us from starting at all, and we never would have known the magic we were capable of creating. You might only have 60 per cent of the ingredients to start something, but you're *100 per cent ready* to figure everything else out as you go.

We too easily underestimate our own abilities to learn and adapt and forget that many of our skills that seem specific are, in fact, transferable. One of the main areas that holds us back that continues to come up in *Seize the Yay* podcast conversations is how qualified you feel to be doing what you're doing. I know in my case, while I have since discovered that my many years of legal training are quite transferable to business, not having any experience or entrepreneurial training initially felt like a huge obstacle. Before launching Matcha Maiden, I even considered doing an MBA to prepare myself, and that would have taken at least a year, if not several, preventing us from taking advantage of the perfect timing we ended up launching into.

 You might only have 60 per cent of the ingredients to start something, but you're *100 per cent ready* to figure everything else out as you go.

Though I am grateful for the years of schooling I had, I always come back to the many examples that show me that formal study is *not* a necessary ingredient for success, whether in the area you want to move towards or just a technical qualification in general. There are countless famous examples of college-dropouts-turned-success-stories in industries you might think would require degrees. You might be surprised to hear these include people such as Mark Zuckerberg, Bill Gates and Steve Jobs. In business at least, and many other industries, there is so much you can learn by *doing*, especially in a climate where things are changing so rapidly and drastically that even those with current qualifications will soon find them outdated.

And so, you can see how much getting anything done is just a mind game with yourself. Whenever I'm asked about my tips for success, after I remind myself that I *am* qualified to answer that question, I always come back to having learned how to better direct my mind and trick it out of its destructive tendencies. I cannot even tell you the number of times I've faked it 'til I maked it (sounds way better, right?), or how many times I know I'll continue to do so in the future. Consider this strategy a little security blanket for you to hold onto as you take those first shaky steps out of the nurturing clutches of your comfort zone.

CHAPTER 4

Comparison is the thief of joy

Given the prevalence of the fake it 'til you make it methodology, you would think that comparing your way to yay with someone else's progress wouldn't even cross your mind because you know it might not be real anyway. Often, the journey we *perceive* someone to be on is not necessarily the one they are on at all. So given that what we see of others on the surface is often their projected or feigned confidence, comparison with them is illogical and futile. Not only are no two of us the same, but no two of us are on the same journey. And yet, one of the most common grievances I hear from people, particularly women (and especially young women), relates to how their face/body/career/partner/freckle distribution compares to others.

Comparison is the thief of so much joy (or the thief of yay, in your brand-new vernacular), but even so, I suspect many of you still find yourself wrapped up in its web from time to time – I know I do. I will openly admit, again, that even after growing both of our matcha businesses and the *Seize the Yay* podcast beyond my wildest dreams, I still spiral into worry sometimes about how our success and trajectory match up to others, and even how I personally match up to people around me. This is particularly the case during speaking opportunities or on other occasions where I'm asked to share our journey. I'll often find myself getting bogged down in a rather destructive inner dialogue: *Is my story interesting enough? Aren't there better speakers with more interesting insights who could be doing this instead of me?* But then, eventually, the realisation comes that I wouldn't be there at all if somebody out there didn't find our story interesting – our story is the one I've been asked to tell.

Almost every person I've interviewed for my podcast – from incredibly successful and/or famous people to quiet achievers – has surprised me by admitting that they still fall into the comparison trap and allow those thoughts to detract from their own very real and admirable achievements. If you've listened to my podcast, you'll know that after the segment where we discuss my guest's 'way to yay' comes a segment called 'nay to yay', in which they detail the major barriers they've encountered on their way to finding joy. In more cases than I ever anticipated, self-doubt has emerged as the most pervasive theme, followed closely by social comparison. The old adage, 'The grass is always greener on the other side' reminds us that things always look better from afar, but I'm not sure it entirely equips us for the constant barrage of perfectly manicured bright green lawns (both literally and figuratively) that roll onto our screens in this modern digital age.

I am a great lover of social media and the platform it provides for community building and connection through ideas. It has democratised influence in a big way and made it possible for people like me to engineer massive life changes off the back of a single good idea. Advancements in the digital world have also made it possible for me to leave an office job behind and work from wherever seems appropriate at the time. I'll continue to blow social media's horn for this reason: it has contributed to me seizing my yay and building a yay-bourhood.

This world of connectivity does, however, have many downsides; one of which is the visibility of everyone else's lives. Never before has our culture encouraged the splashing around of every detail of our daily lives with complete strangers as strongly as it does today. We humans (understandably) like to put our best foot forward in any public interactions, but those interactions have suddenly become a 24/7 rolling live feed of highlights. Even if you live a relatively analogue life (although even my mum has discovered the joys of a good old Facebook tangent), it is our natural inclination to look at the lives of others as a sort of benchmark for our own. And if social media is, in fact, simply being used as a benchmark for inspiration, then comparison can absolutely be a healthy motivator or instigator for change. The problem occurs when we take comparison much further than this, with potentially destructive results.

Seize your pay

Before we go further, I want to emphasise that not all social comparison is negative. It can be used to your advantage in certain situations. I've looked to others for positive guidance and inspiration throughout all stages of my journey, both in my legal career and in business. When I worked at the law firm, I was probably even a little *under*-comparative in some areas, especially when it came to industry wages, and this ended up working against me.

Having come straight from university into a position where having a salary at all felt like riches, I didn't think to compare my pay packet with anyone else's. I was grateful to have landed the job that I did at a time when top-tier positions were increasingly scarce. I was also brought up in a family that believed that money, religion and politics were impolite topics of conversation, so it didn't occur to me to do any subtle research into what colleagues or friends doing similar work were getting paid. For a few years, this unwillingness to compare actually put me at quite a disadvantage in negotiations and annual reviews because I had no benchmark for what was reasonable for my level of experience.

In many law firms or other corporations, it's common for graduate-level lawyers to start with uniform pay increases. These only start to vary a few years later when they become experienced enough for their performance to meaningfully differ. A combination of naivety, discomfort with asking what anyone else was getting paid and general difficulty putting a value on myself meant that I didn't even know when our pay had started to vary. This prevented me from having a chance to negotiate for an increase during my performance reviews. Had I stayed in that career, over time this could have meant years of lagging behind my peers financially. This is a tragically common scenario, particularly among female professionals despite the incredible pool of talent making it into executive roles.

An enhanced sense of gratitude is admirable in many ways, but, as Sheryl Sandberg mentions in *Lean In*, knowing things could be worse shouldn't stop us from trying to make them better. Career progression often depends on advocating for yourself, but these are traits that women are discouraged from displaying. So there are definitely some instances where comparison can be a useful and reasonable tool that absolutely should be drawn on in order to make sure you are truly asking for what you are worth. The difficulty is learning to navigate that delicate balance between dialogue you can use to your advantage and dialogue that tips you into a negative comparison spiral.

Stopping the spiral

Even though comparison has its uses in some situations, as we've just explored, too many of us take it much further than is reasonable. We benchmark too often and are left feeling worthless, defeated or insignificant after a mindless social media scrolling session. It's a little bit like that incredibly hot but emotionally toxic person we've all gone after in our time: even though you're fully aware of the likely disastrous outcome, you're recklessly determined to pursue them anyway. Even though I know all this, I still often catch myself on a comparison binge.

In *Happy, Healthy, Strong*, Rachael Finch talks about how we have been in competition all our lives: sperm fighting to get to the egg, children fighting for top marks at school, and then adults competing to be better, faster, prettier, smarter or richer than others. Relevantly, she reminds us that constantly trying to outdo or outshine others can only lead to disappointment, toxic relationships and jealousy.

I've been very conscious of falling victim to this comparison trap, particularly since moving into a career that requires me to spend a lot of time on social media observing what others in the market are doing. Knowing that this new level of visibility could be a challenge to adapt to, I decided to tackle this head on rather than wait for it to subtly eat away at my happiness and confidence.

I realised that excessive social comparison was futile for two very key reasons:

1. You are only seeing what other people choose to *let* you see.
2. Even if what you see of their life does look great, how will wallowing over their life do anything to improve yours?

I Post-it-noted these two reasons all over my desk and walls to disrupt negative thoughts if I started to get distracted by them. I also wanted to remind myself that comparison is, as Nic loves to say, as useless as tits on a bull. So now, even if I do still catch myself comparing negatively, there's a built-in circuit breaker. Like I keep saying, it's all about hacking your own thought processes and redirecting them towards your yay.

Expectation vs. reality

I have been reminded many times about the difference between perception and reality, in both directions. And this reinforces how silly it is to waste my energy or time evaluating other people's situations, especially if doing that leaves me feeling crappy about myself, my work or my life.

One thing that I always remind myself of when I want to get perspective is a list of competitors in the matcha space that Nic and I compiled when the market started to become crowded. You'll recall that I started out very much the overthinker and lover of the certainty provided by data. True to that, I used to closely monitor their every move then spend hours updating our comparison spreadsheet, which measured our sizing, pricing, number of products, shipping locations and everything else you can think of against multiple other matcha retailers. Sometimes, we'd even change our minds about a major operational decision based on this comparative exercise and the limited information we had about what others in the market were doing.

Of course, it is important to have some understanding of the landscape you're working in – this is another example of reasonable benchmarking. But letting the moves of others dictate your otherwise reasonable and well-thought-out decisions is a dangerous path to go down. A competitor that drew a lot of our attention over the space of a few years was one we believed to be a business a similar size to ours, if not bigger, based in England. When we set up warehouses in the United States, we decided not to set up a warehouse in the United Kingdom, fearing that this particular business already had too strong a hold on the market. Years later, the owners wanted to sell their business and they ended up approaching us to buy it. Nic and I were pleasantly surprised to learn that their recent yearly sales were less than ours had been *per month*, but we were also frustrated by how much we had let their presence in the market affect us.

The flip side of overestimating another business is under-estimating how others might see you. A business we have always looked up to is T2, which was acquired by food and FMCG giant Unilever in 2013. In addition to their extensive tea offering, T2 also entered the matcha market around the same time we did. They added several matcha-based products to their broader offering, which was of a size and volume across the country that we felt precluded us from even trying to compete. We started to actively ignore the direction they were taking in matcha, believing that because of our more niche health and wellness angle we were operating in completely different spheres, and that it wouldn't matter what we did because we were far too small to interact with a business like that in any way.

Thankfully, we didn't make any negative decisions based on this assumption, because – as we found out later – it was wrong. On two separate occasions, we talked to T2 CEOs (one current, one former), and each told us that Matcha Maiden was well known to the team and definitely on their radar as a market player. There we were, thinking we'd have to introduce our business from scratch and that they would never have heard of us, only to find out these giants considered us as big enough to warrant consideration in executive meetings. I'm sure we've been in many other situations that illustrate this same point of flawed comparisons leading to time and energy being misplaced.

In a more personal context, there are countless examples of people who have seemingly 'perfect' lives later revealing trauma or other personal challenges that nobody knew anything about. If you ever need proof that money and success aren't the answers to life, simply look to Hollywood. It may be too soon to say, but at the time of writing this, it seems we are all searching for a little more authenticity and well-roundedness in the content we are consuming, which would be wonderful for the digital landscape. But even if we start moving in that direction, there will always be those in the digital world and the real world who present themselves in a way that omits their flaws, challenges or downsides. This is absolutely a personal choice and may be based on many factors in that person's life. But it doesn't do the rest of us any favours in preventing a crisis of worthiness by comparison to their seemingly perfect exterior.

As frustrating as this might be, it is not on us to change other people's behaviour, but it is on us to work on changing the way we respond to it internally (if we respond to them at all). Your energy and efforts are precious and limited resources; why spend them anywhere but on your own journey? Even if the way someone presents their life isn't convoluted or calculated, there are always things sitting just below the surface – private battles or struggles we will never know the half of. The most outwardly 'together' among us have faced (or are still facing) the most challenging obstacles. My very wise mum always taught me to be kind to everyone, for you never know the struggles they are facing behind closed doors. She also taught me to be careful what you wish for because you never know the totality of what that coming true might involve.

Your energy and efforts are precious and limited resources; why spend them anywhere but on your own journey?

Take, for example, one of my dear friends Olivia Molly Rogers, who was literally named one of the most beautiful people in Australia and crowned Miss Universe Australia in 2017. When you add this to her academic qualifications as a speech pathologist and her natural talents as a self-taught artist, her life seems outwardly perfect. Throughout the pageant, Olivia exuded confidence, motivation and drive, and ultimately ended up winning the title. And yet, while recording my first live *Seize the Yay* show, she generously shared with me that at that time, and during her subsequent rise to fame, she was only just starting to recover from a crippling, long-term eating disorder and the associated diagnoses of anxiety and depression.

Her anxiety and depression still flare up from time to time, but Olivia is now a dedicated advocate and passionate ambassador for mental health and authenticity on social media. She regularly shares these 'behind the scenes' insights into her life for the benefit of others, making an invaluable contribution to the social media landscape.

My own way to yay has also been riddled with behind-the-scenes struggles. The periods where my anxiety has been at its worst, for example, are times where I was least likely (or able) to discuss what was going on behind closed doors – even if I was later able to be open about them. At the same time my body crashed with adrenal fatigue under the pressure of the gut parasite I brought home from Africa, I also experienced somewhat of a mental crash, triggering severe anxiety and panic attacks. In part, being so severely underweight led my body into panic mode, but this also came off the back of a prolonged, traumatic family separation, which my body was finally starting to process. I had never experienced proper anxiety before, having always believed people suffering from it should simply 'chill out' or get a massage. Looking back, however, I realised I had experienced several panic attacks throughout my life without knowing it, and that this late-onset anxiety was probably here to stay.

Fast-forward to the second half of 2016, by which time I had long-since recovered from the parasite and both of our two businesses were performing wonderfully. I was fully embracing the funtrepreneur life and living the wellness dream. That was, however, until my second major burnout – as I've mentioned, I used to be slow on the uptake when it came to my health. This time, I was so in love with our work and getting so carried away with the lack of structure that I forgot to take a break. It was at this point that I realised you *can* have too much of a good thing. I finally understood that burnout can be triggered not only by physical overstimulation, but also by excess emotional and mental stimulation.

I also learned that even 'fun' things are still work: going to events and catching up for work meetings didn't feel like my legal work used to, but they still required lots of mental effort and energy. I didn't know it at the time, but this was where the first seeds were sown for the idea of 'play' and the importance of *emotional* rest and not just physical rest.

After almost two years without a day off, I ended up with such severe anxiety that I was bedridden and largely unable to attend events, work effectively or interact with friends and family as my true self. And yet, for those several months of being unwell, my social media accounts were full of smiley throwbacks and filler content (or no content at all).

My posts revealed very little to my followers until much later, when I had recovered enough to discuss my problems openly. Even many of my closest friends and our key staff were unaware that anything was wrong until then. Not because I wanted to hide it – I'm a devoted oversharer in the name of authenticity – but because I simply didn't have the energy to explain. If you had been comparing yourself to me at that time and basing your ideas about me on how things *appeared* to be, you would have been comparing against a completely skewed reality and wasting a whole heap of time and energy in the process. The only reality you have a real insight into and have to live out each day is your own. That's where your focus, love and energy should be channelled.

  The only reality you have a real insight into and have to live out each day is your own. That's where your focus, love and energy should be channelled.

The grass is greenest where you water it

The reality is no matter how great your life is, there will always be someone who is richer, more successful, happier or healthier than you (no matter which metric you measure by) because not everything in life is fair and equal. In very few cases will we ever actually be the worldwide 'best' at something (if you are, please feel free to skip right on past this section), but the most liberating realisation for me has been that I don't *have* to be the 'best' to live an entirely fulfilled, meaningful and exciting life.

Since the only person's life that you live day-to-day is your own, making that the best it can be ought to be your main focus. If you dwell on the macro-level questions about who is doing better or where you are in relation to your peer group, you draw your energy away from the micro-level details that shape the depth and quality of your day-to-day experience. A quote that I love is one that Steph Claire Smith and Laura Henshaw chose as their favourite on the podcast (the question every episode finishes on): 'Don't compare your life to others. There's no comparison between the sun and the moon, they each shine when it's their time.' These two best friends beautifully illustrate how powerful we can be when we focus our attention on celebrating each other instead of comparing ourselves.

Because they're both young, health-focused, fitness-loving models, Steph and Laura might once have been considered competitors or even rivals, and they could easily have been caught up in comparing themselves to one another. Instead, they joined forces to create Keep It Cleaner, a booming empire that started with an e-book and now includes an app, food range, podcast, book and bustling community. Not only have these two managed to side-step comparison, they've taken it one step further and harnessed the power of collaboration while also maintaining their individual identities and projects outside of Keep It Cleaner. Focusing their attention on celebrating each other and their own unique talents, personalities and skill sets rather than measuring them up against each other has borne more fruits than comparison ever would have done.

As anyone who's ever tried to go to the gym in winter knows, motivation can be a terribly volatile state of mind as it is, so fuelling any negativity with comparison is not only useless but can send you backwards. Our energy is a preciously limited resource that is already spread thin by the pace and density of our lives, so using it up by poring over other people's lives seems a wasteful thing to do, as that is only going to borrow energy from other things that you care about. That precious time and energy currency should be invested where it will have the most impact in the details of your own life. Whether others are living theirs better, worse or the same as you may be relevant to the extent of providing a benchmark or inspiration for you, but shouldn't be allowed to creep far enough into your mind that it detracts from the highs, lows and learnings of your own pathyay (or in fact takes the yay out of it altogether).

 That precious time and energy currency should be invested where it will have the most impact in the details of your own life.

I won't deny that I still find myself caught up in the uncertainty and feelings of unworthiness that follow any comparison binge from time to time. These binges can completely strip me of motivation, confidence and excitement for the amazing life I get to live for hours or even a whole day. In fact, that's exactly why I'm at such pains to emphasise how destructive excessive comparison to others can be, wasting precious hours that could have been spent full of action, productivity or joy. I've experienced how this energy expenditure ultimately affects nobody else except me, and then takes so much work to pull myself out of. Just like self-doubt, the temptation to compare will probably never leave you completely, so it is crucial to be able to recognise it immediately and develop the tools to shut it down before you spiral out of control and lose sight of the things that *do* matter. I am realising more and more how strictly we need to exercise our ability to choose where our mind goes in order to end up where we want to be.

Blinker your way to yay

It's probably never been harder *not* to compare yourself to others given how much we all share of our goings-on, but I think it is possible to wean ourselves from the addiction of social comparison. I have spent the past few years refining my own practice, particularly as Nic and I have moved further and further into the world of social media.

There is, as with any 'addiction', always the possibility of relapsing from time to time into a comparison binge. I wasted half a day this week with my stomach in knots feeling totally inadequate because I indulged in a stalking session in order to compare myself to someone else. It is such a yucky, sinking feeling and it really does unnecessarily take the joy away from your achievements and endeavours. But even if we aren't completely immune to the comparison trap, we can at least limit its discouraging and destructive impact with the right tools.

I have developed a little tactic I like to call my 'blinkered approach' based on the leather blinkers racehorses wear to block out the rest of the field, allowing that horse to focus purely on the finish line. Day to day, this translates to a very *heavy* curation of the world around me – both in social media and in real life. Just like any other naughty habit or addiction, social comparison is a behaviour that is generally triggered by something. One of the main underlying steps to seizing the yay is understanding that we have far more choice over our circumstances, and that life does not so much happen *to* us as happen because of the choices we make. If we choose to indulge the triggers in our environment, then we are also choosing to buy into the cycle of comparison, self-doubt and crappyness that can follow. At the same time, that means we can choose to shut out or 'blinker' ourselves against the triggers that surround us and thereby limit the impact we allow these behaviours to have on our lives.

Personal blinkers

Blinkering as a strategy sounds simple, and yet it has taken me an alarmingly long time to realise that I can blinker myself by removing negative influences so that they don't impact me as easily. For me, as I imagine is the case for many of you, social media is the main breeding ground for my comparative tendencies, so that's the area I have had to curate the most dramatically. Most of us probably follow accounts for people or businesses that evoke a sense of inadequacy or give us a little stab in the stomach, even if we can logically appreciate how silly that is. Since I was a child, I have been relatively good at separating my own worth from that of others, but even still, I could whip you up a pretty quick list of accounts that trigger me into comparing myself in a negative way.

Whether you measure yourself against others in the looks, body, career or relationship department, you can blinker those areas in order to filter out the discouraging effect they have on your confidence and motivation. I know at least among my friends, we tend to be much better at curating our real-life surroundings to limit things that make us feel bad (although not in all cases), but not as good at applying this curating to our digital environment. I have become much stricter over the past few years at unfollowing or simply muting accounts that trigger those questioning feelings in me or distract me from my work, passions and joy. This has involved a bit of juggling between my desire to stay connected and keep up with what people are doing on one hand and needing to protect my self-worth on the other hand, but part of the blinkers approach for me is always choosing self-worth first.

You might not always need these kinds of measures. There might just be certain times in your life where they feel more necessary than others. Our wedding, for example, was a time when I was more sensitive than usual about making the right choices among a literal ocean of options. I was probably more prone to comparing myself physically to other brides. Who doesn't want to look and feel their best for their big day?

 Part of the blinkers approach for me is always choosing self-worth first.

Prior to this, there was, of course, a wonderful phase of information gathering. I sought inspiration from other beautiful weddings and went to town on my Pinterest account as I started getting excited about crafting our special day. But once we started to make final decisions and lock things in, it became very hard not to see new ideas pop up and become dissatisfied with what we had chosen. My bridesmaids will have a good giggle remembering how much I absolutely adored the process of creating the incredible custom Pallas Couture gown I was lucky enough to wear on the day, only to have a breakdown in the final week because I'd looked at too many other dresses. Sensibly, they barred me from any social media that week, and by the wedding day, I'd fallen in love with my dress all over again. You need to be happy with what is right for you and remember it's got nothing to do with anyone else's choices.

Remember, you don't need to block things out forever, you only need to identify when they might trigger you unproductively and work out how to arm yourself against that. I find, for example, that when I haven't had much time for exercise or eating as healthily as I usually like to, I'm likely to get more drawn into other people's bodies or fitness levels than I usually would. So, I need to be more careful about scrolling mindlessly on social media during these times. When I have been able to maintain a great wellness routine, nothing really bothers me, so those are the times the blinkers can come off and I can stalk away to my heart's content.

You don't need to block things out forever, you only need to identify when they might trigger you unproductively.

I also found this approach useful during my legal career to filter things out of my working environment that could interrupt my focus or productivity. A beloved topic of gossip in most workplaces is the intricacies of everyone else's careers and who's getting promoted, poached or doing anything interesting or out of the ordinary. The best thing you can do to avoid any negative self-talk or fallout from this kind of information is to avoid getting involved in the chat to begin with. In my experience, the gossip corners of the office are well-known to everyone, so you'll be easily able to identify the spots to avoid if you're having a less emotionally resilient day or period than usual and don't want to hear it.

Business blinkers

We've also applied this blinkered approach to business over time to help block out things that might trigger unhelpful doubts or worry. From our social media accounts for Matcha Maiden and then Matcha Mylkbar, while we were initially one of the only competitors in the landscape, as new entrants began to pop up, I'd follow every single one and trawl through their content very closely. This very quickly resulted in me losing large chunks of time analysing what they might be doing and trying to deduce from what they were posting what their levels of success might be. Each time we would hit a milestone or achieve something exciting, there would be a measuring up exercise going on in the back of my mind that would adjust my level of joy accordingly rather than celebrating each event for its independent value.

Early on, we appointed wonderful distributors for Matcha Maiden in several states, but had been hoping to strike a deal with one of the biggest, national distributors in Australia. After many months of pitches, sampling and negotiations, we finally got the deal over the line – more than tripling our product distribution. We should have been overjoyed and excited about this huge step forwards, but then we found out that they'd signed a competing matcha supplier on board just months earlier, before they found out about us. Our products were positioned very differently towards different segments of the market, which had, in any case, exploded enough to allow room for both of us, but we allowed our excitement to be completely deflated.

Nowadays, I can see that this was a hugely positive sign for the direction of the matcha market overall, and the arrangements we have with this distributor have proven enormously beneficial for both matcha brands. By getting sidetracked and comparing our product with theirs, Nic and I lost out on a beautiful opportunity for celebration. The blinkered approach to business took me a few years to fully develop as I slowly realised the damaging impact comparison was having on our own experience of business. Ultimately, I ended up unfollowing or muting all the accounts that detracted from the things that were going amazingly in our own world.

Though it makes sense to have some understanding of what your competitors are doing, I had to make a call that it was better to know less and compare less than to know more and drown in a sea of emotion. Blinkering those distractions allowed me to put my head down and focus on the only thing I had control over: the effort Nic and I were putting into our own business and giving it what it needed to continue growing. As years went by and we became more confident in our own achievements, I slowly started to re-introduce a lot of the information I had filtered out, only this time I knew it would not result in a comparative spiral. Just like personal blinkers, you can whip them out when you need them most and retire them once you're more confident in your ability to resist the comparison trap.

Real-world blinkers

This same heavy curation is available in the real world, too. An environmental example of being overly comparative is writing this book. A (not insignificant) part of me was reluctant to write a book without first reading every other book of a similar genre written on similar topics for 'reference' and 'research'. In other words, I wanted to compare my ideas with other authors and decide whether my ideas were worthy of publication.

Instead, once I knew this book was really going to happen, I ended up reading a grand total of zero related books. Any books I've referred to in these pages were read long before I knew I would write my own. By now, I know myself well enough to know how distracted and discouraged I would have felt every time I encountered something I'd either taken an opposite view on, hadn't included in my book or simply hadn't written as eloquently. So I simply removed that risk altogether.

Other authors might not take this same approach; they might be very comfortable drawing guidance from the writings of others as they craft their own books. However, I knew very early on that I had to return to my blinkering approach in order to keep focused, motivated and confident enough to press on. It might sound a bit reckless to advise you to simply turn a blind eye to relevant information around you, but I can only speak to what's been helpful for me. I truly believe that if you know information could be more harmful than helpful, it's better to block it out altogether – at least until you're mentally prepared for it.

Similarly, my earlier advice about starting before you're ready and ripping off the bandaid might also seem a bit irresponsible. But again, I believe that a hasty and even messy start is better than never starting at all. The unruliness of this kind of spontaneous approach is perhaps why it's so powerful; it allows your mind to shut off obstructive overthinking so you can get on with the important things that will move you forward. Seizing your yay is more about mastering your mind than anything else. For me, compartmentalising with blinkers is a huge part of the game.

 Seizing your yay is more about mastering your mind than anything else.

Reframe the comparison

Rather than focusing on what others are doing, something I've also found helpful is to swap social comparison for temporal comparison. This is similar to one of the techniques we mentioned when talking about journalling. Instead of comparing myself to anyone else, I simply compare what I'm doing now with what I was doing at an earlier time. After all, comparing yourself with your earlier self is really the only legitimate comparison you can make.

Since entering the podcast world, I could easily have become distracted and disheartened by the technical proficiency, millions of downloads and guest lists of other podcasters. I could have wasted my time lamenting my inability to ever catch up (I'll openly admit, this has crossed my mind a few times). However, a far more productive comparison is to look back at the total noob I was when I recorded my first episode. Doing this gives me so much progress to celebrate. I have since learned so much about audio production and editing, I've welcomed guests I would never have dreamed of interviewing and have now been around for over a year, meaning others are probably now feeling that same 'I'll-never-catch-up' feeling about my podcast. Reframing the comparison this way is so much more joyful and positive.

Defuse the comparison bomb

Another way to reframe comparison, for me, is by doing what feels like the scariest thing in order to defuse the comparison trigger. A great example of this has to do with body image, which is a sore point for many women. Negative body image doesn't plague or consume me like it does some people, for which I feel very fortunate, but it does still strike me from time to time – I am a woman, after all. With images of perfect bodies constantly at our fingertips, it is so easy for us to beat ourselves up about the way we look.

Newsflash: we are all composed of completely different genetic make-ups, lifestyles and environmental factors, so we are not meant to look the same as each other. With my Asian heritage, my body (which I lovingly refer to as that of a 12-year-old boy) is never going to have voluptuous curves or cleavage, and I'd look ridiculous if it did. But the upside is that I can run without a bra *and* wear sack dresses. You win some, you lose some.

I have nonetheless caught myself measuring my body against those of stunning, sculpted models whose literal job it is to take care of their physical appearance. They spend all day in pursuit of that end, while I, in contrast, am squeezing fitness in wherever I can between running three businesses and other random work (none of which requires me to look a certain way). I keep bringing myself back to an apples and oranges analogy: what sense is there in comparing when we are living completely different lives? I wouldn't be willing to do what they do for their bodies anyway.

Instead, I return to temporal comparison and try to measure myself against where I currently am and what I know to be my fittest, healthiest body. Another thing I do is try to have a little laugh at the situation and lighten the serious comparative mood. Something that has worked wonders for my confidence and killed my temptation to compare (in the weirdest way) is a little exercise I call 'bloops'. I used to find myself agonising over getting the perfect photo to post on social media – one that 'measured up' to everyone else's, but then I realised how much time and emotional energy I was wasting on this process. I would end up posting photos that reflected only one take of the 2,039,823 takes that didn't make the cut.

So, one day, along with posting a nice, edited photo I decided to also post the *worst*, most goober-like photo I could find – the image I was *least* comfortable with sharing. Again, this was all about ripping off the bandaid and forcing myself to relax about the whole thing. A benefit to this approach was that I would be more authentic in the content I was sharing. Though putting up that first bloop felt so scary, I now love sharing those blooper posts: eyes half-shut, mouth half-open, stomach bloated, camel toe on show . . . It's all fair game! I feel more comfortable doing this than I do posting my posed, professional highlights. The thing that surprised me more than the affirming, positive responses

I got from people was how adopting this practice affected my relationship with myself: it's made me much less harsh on myself and far more comfortable in my body from *all* angles.

A woman I adore for her work in the space of body image and body confidence is Taryn Brumfitt, founder of the Body Image Movement and director of the documentary *Embrace*. Nothing has hit me quite so poignantly in helping me learn to love my body for the miracle it is than Taryn's work. As she likes to regularly remind us, 'Your body is not an ornament, it is the vehicle to your dreams!' After giving birth to her third child, Taryn experienced feelings of loathing for her body, and seriously considered cosmetic surgery. She settled on a tummy tuck, boob job and liposuction and booked herself in for surgery. A few weeks later, she pulled out – worried about the impact it could have on her daughter.

Instead, Taryn decided to get herself in top physical shape by entering a female body-building competition. She worked tirelessly to lose 15 kilograms in as many weeks and get herself looking the best she ever had. When competition day came, however, she ultimately found the experience of being judged uncomfortable and felt no closer to accepting her body. Later, she eased off on her training and even threw out the scales, gradually learning to accept herself exactly as she was.

She was undoing what she calls the 'brainwashing' that led to her thinking her body had to look a particular way to be beautiful. As part of that process, Taryn posted a before-and-after photo that blew up the internet by flipping the typical slim-down before-and-after photo on its head. Her before photo was her competition-ready, ab-tastic self while the after was a nude self-portrait of a more voluptuous, much happier person. More than 200 million people saw the photographs, and 7000 emails poured into her inbox to thank her for redefining the way we think about our bodies.

This response encouraged her to start a Kickstarter campaign to fund her ground-breaking body image documentary, *Embrace*, which has since become Australia's most successful crowdfunded documentary. Her campaign and film have been supported by the likes of Ashton Kutcher, Ricki Lake and Rosie O'Donnell for its incredibly powerful message on our conditioning towards our bodies. I can't recommend a film more highly to help combat the harsh tendencies we have towards our bodies (and ourselves generally). Taryn is now in the process of crowdfunding again to produce another documentary, *Embrace Kids*.

The more you can surround yourself with uplifting content like this, with diverse views, the better your mind is equipped to resist the negative spirals that comparison can spark. Of course, there's always going to be temptation to compare ourselves to the bodies, careers, success and lives of others. Like addressing any other destructive habit, it's not about expecting yourself to become completely immune, but rather learning to flip the dialogue productively, and as quickly as you can. We were never meant to be the same as each other and our differences are both necessary and inevitable. You can choose to lament those differences or celebrate them for the things that make you special and unique. I spent my youth trying to pad my bras and otherwise conceal my differences to conform, but I now try to own the quirks and characteristics that make me different, and I've never been happier in who I am.

 It's not about expecting yourself to become completely immune, but rather learning to flip the dialogue productively, and as quickly as you can.

Adopt an attitude of gratitude

The best antidote to negativity is gratitude. Much like combating self-doubt by focusing on the reasons why you *are* skilled and capable of making things work, focusing on what you are grateful for can help combat the things you're lamenting that you're not. I often remind myself that someone else out there is dreaming of having something I take for granted, and this can really help me gain perspective on things I'm fretting over unnecessarily. But even without flipping the comparison, gratitude isn't necessarily about whether your situation is better or worse than someone else's; it's about simply being thankful for what you have in and of itself.

Regardless of what anyone else has, there are countless things you could observe in your life that you have or that you are to be grateful for. Many people have taken to gratitude journalling as a big part of their wellbeing practice. Even though being adopted doesn't come up as often as you'd think in my life, when I'm practising gratitude, I always come back to it. I did nothing to warrant special treatment or deserve a chance at the life I have versus the one I was born into (I was only a six-month-old blob at the time, after all), and yet my parents came to give me an incredible life in Australia. So now, every part of living here is something to be grateful for. This sense of appreciation flows on to include the amazing, supportive family and friends Nic and I are surrounded by who fill our lives with joy and depth, and have played instrumental roles in making us who we are.

The importance of gratitude has perhaps never been so starkly clear as during the coronavirus pandemic that hit the world in the very last stages of finishing this book. While we would never wish for such tragic events to teach us a lesson, I think it came as a timely reminder to many of us to appreciate the smaller, simpler things in life and not to take anything or anyone for granted. Try taking some time out each day to write down your own list of things you are grateful for. This could be anything from the roof over your head, your able body and mind, or the friendships you are surrounded by. Even in times as challenging as global social isolation, we can be grateful for modern innovations like FaceTime and Zoom that still allow us to stay in touch. Things as small as being able to move freely without pain, speak easily without impediment or see clearly without obstruction are things to be grateful for. The miracle of our bodies makes our harsh comparison of their external shell seem silly.

The things you are grateful for could be even smaller and more trivial than this, but they are still worthy of acknowledging or writing down: your coffee in the morning or the cute dog down the street that plays with you. (To everyone in our neighbourhood, Paul says 'you're welcome'.) It doesn't have to be a grand, completely life-changing event to spark gratitude, it can be small and simple. The things you're grateful for don't even have to be positive things. There might be difficult or challenging situations in your life that highlight things you appreciate or that teach you lessons you are grateful for.

You can see how focusing your attention on all the great things in your life can help move you away from the throes of negative comparison. One of the people who inspires me most in this world is Dave 'Barney' Miller, who was a guest on the podcast along with his wife, Kada. Both of them embody the art of gratitude and appreciating all we have in life. Barney is a world surfing champion but, unlike your average surfing champion, he is also a quadriplegic.

In 1999, at the age of 20, Barney was a promising young surfer when a tragic car accident led to him being airlifted to hospital where he was pronounced dead on arrival. He woke up in hospital to be told he was a complete C6 quadriplegic and he would never breathe independently again or use his right arm. His unwavering resolve and deep sense of gratitude to be alive saw him through intense rehabilitation. And this, in turn, has since led him to not only breathe independently and use his right arm, but also get back in the water to his beloved surfing – often assisted by best mate, Mick Fanning.

Barney met Kada eight years later, when they both pulled each other out of difficult times. Through their shared commitment to his rehab, he was even able to kneel to propose to Kada and stand at the altar at their wedding. In 2017, Barney fulfilled his dream of becoming a world surfing champion, taking out the title at the inaugural US Adaptive Surfing Championship and then the ISA World Adaptive Surf Championship. Barney and Kada have both faced more challenge and tragedy than most – together and separately. Even so, they never lament, 'Why us?' Instead, they focus their energy perpetually on gratitude.

In the very first chapter of their book, *The Essence of You and Me*, their joint words reveal the strength of their mindset very clearly. 'We tend to live in a world of pure imagination . . . [in] that we believe in every fibre of our cells that we have the ability to influence our life experience through our thoughts, choices and perception.' Barney and Kada's resolute, unwavering ability to look at the bright side of life is a constant source of inspiration to me.

I don't include their story so that you start comparing yourself to Barney and Kada (though I, too, have done this – I'm in awe of their strength). Thinking about what others have to endure compared to us is still a cognitive measurement of how we stack up against someone else; it's just a downward comparison instead of an upwards one. Rather, I mention their story to show them as an example of the practice of gratitude in two people who do it so well. True gratitude – the kind that can help combat comparative thinking – is based more on our relationship with ourselves and how we feel about our own circumstances.

Staying in a grateful frame of mind keeps your focus squarely on what you *do* have, rather than what you *don't*. And this applies to your work life as well as your personal life. Grab a journal and start writing down some of the things you appreciate in your life. It can be a wonderful tool for clarity, mental health and happiness.

CHAPTER 5

Building your yay-bourhood

While the previous chapter aims to draw you *away* from focusing on competitors or rivals too heavily, I'm now going to say DO focus keenly on your supporters and friends. Curating your surroundings to best facilitate the life you want to live and evaluating your closest relationships is one of the most important steps in seizing your yay.

While it is vitally important to develop the tools to quieten any negative inner chatter independently (some of which we discussed), there is nothing wrong at all with phoning a friend along the way (and I still do it almost every day). It is often said that you can't live a positive life with a negative mind, as we have somewhat covered already, but I also believe you can't live a positive life with a negative *network.* No amount of work on building self-confidence and emotional resilience will withstand the constant disapproval or disparagement from those closest to you or around you most. And so, we come to another one of my all-time favourite pieces of wisdom from Jim Rohn to help you seize your yay: You are the sum of the five people you spend the most time with.

The views, beliefs and values of those closest to you will undoubtedly impact your own and the way those play out in your life. This doesn't necessarily mean the people you literally spend the most minutes with, like the work colleagues you sit with each day whose presence you share without much choice in the matter. For some of you, your immediate family might be a difficult area of life; you can't always distance yourself from them, and they might not always be on board with your direction. Rather, I think this saying is aimed more at the people you *do* have a choice about spending time with, and how you exercise that choice to align your 'top five' with where you want to end up.

 You are the sum of the five people you spend the most time with.

There are so many things I want to say about the importance of the people around you, but above all I'd lean on the famous proverb relating to raising young children, which I believe applies to the process of starting a business or getting any dream off the ground no matter who you are: 'It takes a village to raise a child' (or perhaps brainchild). My upbringing is a perfect example of this. All arms of the family got involved to enable the logistics involved with helping me pursue my many hobbies and interests from childhood all the way through to our businesses, and my family still pitches in heavily to this day.

Both Matcha Maiden and Matcha Mylkbar have also been enriched invaluably from the contribution of those around us. The café in particular combines the skills and perspectives of all four business partners as well as our friends. In every pursuit in your life, building the right village around you will set you in good stead for whatever comes next.

Identify the right yay-bours

Whether the goal you have in mind right now is personal or professional, everything that follows applies to both kinds equally. Many business success stories tend to focus primarily on the founder or original creator of an idea, but in almost every case, that person was supported by a team of people to get to where they ended up – without them, it wouldn't have been possible. Very rarely is success the work of one person; few incredible things are created in a vacuum. Even the mighty Beyoncé takes time to acknowledge her dancers and support performers, and you can only imagine the army of others it must take to make her moments of greatness what they are.

Support can be given in many forms, from tangible things like mentoring or funding to keep you afloat, to moral and emotional support. Whatever their contribution, there are so many other players besides the protagonists in every story, including our own. The people you choose to surround yourself with – the way they interact with your confidence, self-belief, skill set and physical abilities, even financing and networks – will have such a huge impact on how successful or happy you will be. It makes sense that you will want to choose them wisely (and change them wisely) to build out the best village you can to get you to your dream.

For me, leaving law and moving into the world of business required me to go back to basics and reshape a new village to reflect my new dream. I realised how limited my professional circle had become and how my thinking had been shaped accordingly. My former network had served me well during my law career, and that honed ability to think critically remains a treasured skill. But my circle was 90 per cent legal with the remaining 10 per cent mostly in other corporate roles. Suddenly, after Matcha Maiden took off, the people around me who I'd always turned to for advice as a lawyer had little knowledge or experience in the business world I was spending more and more time in. I had never needed such diversity of skills and backgrounds around me but I found myself needing it in all directions immediately if we were to survive. It quickly came time to build a new village for myself, ask for help and figure out who could give it to us.

Even though Nic and I didn't formally hire anyone to join us at Matcha Maiden for quite some time, like many bootstrapped start-ups, the village we built around the business has played a crucial role at every step of the journey. This began with those we could trust and rely on most – our family. We roped them in early on to help keep us afloat, and our fulfilment centre for online orders has been wo-manned by my wonderful aunties Judy and Di for many years, with my mum eventually becoming our full-time wholesale manager. The whole family has rallied around us on many a late night to meet impossible deadlines or help us through times of overwhelm (special mention to honorary 'aunty' Judy Martin). Outside of our family, we then turned to some very talented friends who had skills and experience that we hadn't yet developed. They have been equally generous in sharing them when we needed help.

Brooke Meredith, for example, is the founder and editor-in-chief of the beautiful magazine *A Conscious Collection*, which was a fledgling blog at the time. We've loved growing alongside Brooke's business, and she gave us our first big boost on social media by creating stunning, impeccably presented recipes made with our matcha powder to share with her audience when we didn't have an audience at all. Now, years later, I lend my still-honed legal editing skills to her for the magazine in return. Similarly, Natalie Warner of Greene Street Juice and Sarah Di Iorio of Organika Hair provided the warmest and guiding welcome into the health and wellbeing industry, teaching me the ropes and introducing me to the community. Over the years, we've continued to support each other's businesses in whatever ways we can. I could go on for pages about the many other wonderful friends I've leaned on along the way.

Nic's friendship group was (and still is) equally support-ive. In those scrappy early days of getting Matcha Maiden off the ground, his agency did all our branding and technical infrastructure, and Alan Horn Thomas (a friend who also works for Bushy) has lent his graphic design talents to us many times over. The best man at our wedding, David Higgs, is a leading international photographer, and he has jumped in many times to help us with marketing collateral (including our first, awkwardly posed, promotional headshots). Bodie Czeladka, Nic's business partner at Baroq, went on to build his own SEO and SEM agency, Dilate Digital, which does all our optimisation to this day. And when Nic's long-time friend Glenn Coleman (and his lovely wife Liz) were building their fashion business, Nana Judy, Nic helped with design, marketing and even modelling. Years later, with Nana Judy dominating and hosting Coachella parties with the likes of Rihanna, they returned the favour and gladly helped us with freight forwarding and selling into the United States.

We have been fortunate to be surrounded by so many friends who were already on similar entrepreneurial pathways to us at a similar time. These friends have shared their knowledge, contacts and time, and we've shared back openly. This was just the beginning of the village, or should I say yay-bourhood, we have continued to build around us. Who knows how far we would have gotten if it was only the two of us working on our Matcha Maiden dream. Even if you don't find yourself surrounded by people in positions to help, the way we were, you can always reach out to your networks to find new friends with the skills you need to move forward. Your project or vision might not be entrepreneurial at all – a friend's partner might be the accountant you need advice from, and you could cook them dinner in exchange for an hour of power. Whatever it is you need and can offer in return, there's always a possible exchange that can help you on your way to yay.

Not same, same, but different

Once we'd maxed out the capacity of our very generous friendships, it came time to extend our yay-bourhood in new and different directions. As we had next to no experience, we needed mentoring and expert guidance in almost every area of Matcha Maiden. While I think there's a romance (and simplicity) to seeking out one single mentor to guide you on your way, ultimately, Nic and I ended up 'collecting' multiple mentors across different areas to help where they could – a type of brains trust, if you will. I'd like to pretend we did it all ourselves, but that wasn't the case; name an area of our business and over the years we found a different, incredibly generous go-to person to advise us on it.

Having come from a professionally homogenous environment as a corporate lawyer, what I found to be incredibly important in this process was seeking out a wide range of skills and personalities in the network of people around you. Nic and I, like many others, tended to gravitate towards people who reflected parts of our own personalities or who were on the same wavelength as us, which is hugely important when it comes to feeling aligned or understood.

It is, of course, important to build these like-minded relationships into your network, but in order to use a network most effectively, it is more important to fill gaps in your skills, knowledge and emotional bandwidth, so that you have access to a breadth of perspectives, opinions and experiences. This is especially important in the early days of a small business or new project, when your resources are extremely limited because you can't afford too much overlapping of roles, and you can benefit greatly from a diversity of backgrounds and skills.

I, for example, have finally accepted that I'm an excitable, highly optimistic lover of flowery language who finds the risks, figures and serious stuff a bit of a bore (now that I've left my legal self behind), and this can be inconvenient as a businesswoman. My light-hearted fluffyness has been an asset when it comes to community building, marketing and customer service. However, it's less useful when it comes to debt collecting, negotiations or having hard conversations. Those areas are best addressed by people in our team who operate in a completely different way to me *because* they don't do things the way I do. You aren't always the everything your business (or you) needs, and it's completely okay to acknowledge that. It took me a while to realise, but sometimes your yay-bourhood needs exactly what you are *not*.

Combining diverse skill sets and different personality types proved invaluable once again when, about a year into our Matcha Maiden journey, we had the chance to expand our matcha mission into a physical venue that some of you may know as Matcha Mylkbar.

Remember that story about us packing matcha in a friend's commercial kitchen in the wee hours of the night? Well, that café was Il Fornaio, and it belonged to our long-time friend Mark Filippelli – our first-ever Matcha Maiden stockist. Mark and I studied law together at university, but he tapped out three weeks his law firm career and entered the very different world of hospitality with his older brother Attil to build an incredible empire of venues. It's funny how often networks from lifetimes ago can re-emerge years later in different chapters of our lives. You might be surprised by how many people you already know who have gone off and developed skills or tools that are now useful to you. That's the beauty of investing time in people: it's never a waste. Look around at the people you know, even years ago, and think about how you can bring them into your world.

 You aren't always the everything your business (or you) needs, and it's completely okay to acknowledge that.

In 2015, Mark, Nic and I (now affectionately self-referred to as the three matchateers) happened to be in LA at the same time doing research – Mark into the trends appearing on the food scene and us into the beverage scene, which we ended up choosing to do together. Through our little group circuit of LA's foodie hotspots, we discovered that the two main trends emerging were plant-based eating and matcha drinking. Further digging revealed that the uniting theme underlying those trends was the research being done into 'Blue Zones' – the five areas of the world where people live dramatically longer than anywhere else. The Blue Zone with the most 100-year-olds in the world is Okinawa, Japan, and the longevity of its residents is attributed to a number of factors including plant-based eating and matcha drinking.

It was on this trip during a brainstorming (slightly drunken) dinner date that another 'business plan on a serviette' moment emerged. The three of us decided that we should unite our collective skills to open a longevity-focused, matcha-themed, plant-based café together when we got home. This café would be underpinned by the principles of sustainability, both in terms of longevity and the environment. I mean, who doesn't want the planet and our species to live longer? Instead of focusing on the ethics of farming and eating animals and to take the heat out of the hotly debated vegan scene, we decided we would simply make delicious, filling (and Instagrammable) food without classifying it as vegan and see what people made of it.

Just a few months later, we opened Matcha Mylkbar's doors to the world, and this was only possible because of all the ways we are different and the diversity in the many other people who we called on to help. Mark already had a St Kilda location for an earlier project that had fallen through, so he organised the operational restructure and staffing for our new restaurant. Nic tackled the creative branding and online infrastructure (between jumping on the tools to demolish, paint and plumb, taking him back to his Tassie son-of-a-builder roots). I turned to handling the legal basics and PR. A dear friend jumped in to plan the basic fit-out and a beautiful interior design scheme that we could install quickly *and* within budget. Hundreds of our friends and family members donated their tastebuds, social media audiences, journalistic skills, photography and time to help us get the café open and off to a flying start. This support from our yay-bourhood continues to play an integral role in the business.

Matcha Mylkbar has been open for several years now and we've achieved more than we could ever have dreamed of. As mentioned, the great thing that continues to stand out as a strength of this venture is the way in which each of our unique sets of skills and personalities have united to make this one business a success. We've each brought different learnings gleaned from our existing businesses into this one: Mark has the operational knowledge we could never catch up on, while we have the brand-heavy digital community-building model we used with Matcha Maiden. We all have such different backgrounds, perspectives and ideas to bring to the table and the venue has been a mix of all those from the outset, rather than the result of any one person overriding the direction or decisions. Importantly, none of us were likely to have embarked on this venture independently, but together we were able to take another crazy step into uncharted waters.

Breaking the circle and blind (business) dating

So we've talked about my experiences of building out the yay-bourhood in business, but that doesn't have to be directly related to your work. The past few years have shown me that having a broad range of personalities around you in life *generally* adds a depth to your thinking and the way you approach your life. Amassing an army of people around you that can meet all the various needs you might have as you progress through your way to yay will be your greatest asset because we can't be all things to all people, in all places (although I have tried many times to do so).

Someone once told me that you should never be the smartest person in the room and, if you are, find another room. Everybody knows something that you don't, even if it doesn't seem relevant at the time. It is always my mission to find out what that thing is as soon as possible so that I can learn from the people I am lucky enough to be around. The other thing I've learned is that it's incredibly important to network *before* you actually need it. Building new relationships is never a waste, even if you're not quite sure how they will be immediately useful. The crux of so many decisions and things that happen is based on good relationships, so you can never do yourself a disservice by meeting new people.

To address the elephant in the room before we go any further, I absolutely acknowledge that asking for help or meeting new people is not the easiest thing to do. So, the problem remains as to *how* we go about finding new members of the yay-bourhood, personal or business. There's a special kind of awkwardness reserved for these situations, and there's nothing more cringe-worthy than the awkward hovering we've all done at the edge of a circle that's already deep in conversation, not wanting to interrupt but also wanting to join in so you can get in on the action. The key for me has been owning the awkwardness and just jumping straight into what I call 'breaking the circle', i.e. announcing that you're going to awkwardly join the conversation and laughing off how strange it feels. Everyone understands the feeling, even if they don't show it, and once you've ripped off that bandaid, you can all move on to the bonding and forget it ever happened.

Networking events have been one of my most successful ways to build new friendships, both for work purposes and life generally. I've relied many times on relationships built at events like those of the League of Extraordinary Women, Business Chicks and the like since before I even started my working life (yep, I was that weird law student signing up to professional events before I was a professional, and even did so virtually during isolation). But the thing to get your head around before stepping foot in a new room is that you're only going to get out of those events what you put in. You can walk away without a single new contact or with a stack of business cards that you'll later find incredibly useful, it all depends on how ballsy you're willing to be.

 The crux of so many decisions and things that happen is based on good relationships, so you can never do yourself a disservice by meeting new people.

Similarly, I've sent out many a 'cold-call'-type email to business owners whose brains I've wanted to pick in the hopes that someone would be kind enough to agree to talking with me. Now, I fully understand the eye-roll and heavy sigh that the old 'can I pick your brain?' request can evoke. As scary as it can be approaching a total stranger about your most intimate hopes and dreams, in my experience, people are surprisingly generous and willing to forgo the eye-roll and give you a hand. The small business world in particular seems to be full of that wonderful pay-it-forward type of tradition.

Many times, I've let self-doubt creep in and convince me that others are far too important to respond to little old me, or waste their time helping me out. And yet, the few times I have just gone ahead anyway, I've realised that more often than you'd expect they'll say yes. Or, worst-case scenario, they won't reply, in which case you're in the exact same position as you were before. Although getting a 'no' might feel awkward for about five seconds, it's not the end of the world, and you've lost nothing in the process of trying. And, on the off-chance they say yes, you might just end up with one of your most valuable and cherished contacts.

In the book, *Nice Girls Don't Get the Corner Office*, two chapters prepared me especially well for this kind of networking: 'Don't be too thin-skinned' and '[Don't] not ask questions for fear of sounding stupid'. With lots of practise, I've become a testament to putting yourself out there. I mean, just five years ago, I was in a completely unrelated industry and hadn't heard of (let alone made friends with) many of the wonderful people mentioned in this book. I'm clearly now comfortable with 'putting myself out there'. This technique was truly put to the test a few years back after I wrote an article called, 'Burning the candle at both ends and the middle'. I thought that was such a clever title, and you now know how much it rings true!

The idea for this little article was sparked after reading Arianna Huffington's wonderful book, *Thrive*. I was quite interested in writing some articles for *The Huffington Post* and felt that my article aligned with the tone and content of the platform. On *Thrive's* online portal, Arianna had invited her readers to email her with any contributions. I remember thinking how she probably never expected anyone to take her up on it. I did, however, decide that, as unlikely as a reply would be, I might as well send her the article and see what happened. You can't get what you want if you don't ask for it – shock horror.

I reminded myself that the worst thing she could say was no, or not reply at all. So I sent it, and within a few *hours*, much to my surprise, Arianna replied *personally*. She thanked me for sending her the article and explained how to create a profile to become a contributor to the site in future. Even years later, it still blows my mind that she took the time to reply. A few days later my article was published, and I've continued to contribute articles to *The Huffington Post* since then.

One year I even took this 'who cares if I look silly' attitude to a whole new level, going so far as to organise a string of blind (business) dates to actively expand my networks with people in the very new health and wellness world I was moving into. Many of those who saw past my creepiness and agreed to meet have blossomed into wonderful, long-term relationships. One such example is my dear friend Sally O'Neil (@thefitfoodieblog), who you might know as the woman behind *The Fit Foodie* blog and author of two books, the latest of which is the delightful *The Fit Foodie Meal Prep Plan*. Sally was the very first person I became friends with on the health and wellness scene in Sydney.

We had just started Matcha Maiden at the time and had slowly built out our network among health foodies and fellow health and wellness businesses in Melbourne but had very little contacts up in Sydney, which was an equally important market for us. Sally was (and still is) doing amazing things in the industry, and I thought she would be a great person to spend time with, so I sent her a little Instagram DM when I was in town to ask if she'd like to catch up at a local health food café. We ended up getting along like a house on fire, remaining good friends to this day as well as working together through our businesses many times, even hosting twin events in Melbourne and Sydney giving each other exposure in cities other than our own. I still laugh so much about the fact that none of that would have been possible if I hadn't pushed through the weirdness of approaching her on Instagram.

I'll admit, building your yay-bourhood might not necessarily be easy or quick. It can involve a lot of trial and error as you figure out what skills or traits will best help you on your way, and then go out and find them. You will also learn over time about the best way to approach people when asking for help, as that alone can be quite an art form. As the wonderful Emma Isaacs often says, she takes a gentler 'softly, softly' approach to networking; not asking too much too quickly but simply cultivating strong relationships that bear mutual benefits for both sides over time. And this clearly works because she has relationships with some of the busiest, most successful people in the world. Sometimes, you might get quite a few knock-backs before you ultimately get a yes, but that doesn't mean things won't change down the track.

For example, Emma had a dream to bring Seth Godin, an incredible American author and entrepreneur, to

Australia for a Business Chicks event and it took her eight years to finally get him to agree. As Emma explains in her book, 'I never took Seth's continual dismissals as a personal rejection. To me "no" just means "not now". With each "no" I just saw an opportunity to find more creative ways to get him to say "yes".' There are still many times where I've reached out to others only to find it has ended up in radio silence or a resounding no that discouraged me from trying for eight more years. Often, it will work out, but just as often, if not more so, you end up with a closed door or a curt 'I have to politely decline' type of response.

As I said, these felt awkward and embarrassing for all of a few minutes or a day at most, but then I simply moved on and realised it was worth a try. For all those people who don't say yes to you, there will be so many other people in your close or extended network you reach out to who *will* be willing to lend you an ear or provide a warm introductory email to someone for you. I can't say how often I do this or have this done for me – every single week. Every no just means that isn't one of your people, at least not at this moment in time.

My approach to the cold-call email and 'breaking the circle' have been honed carefully over time, evolving from a more generic but direct request for help to a gentler, more personalised offer to connect to then see what happens from there. I probably started out a little too lawyer-y and direct, asking things straight out rather than investing a little bit of time in the relationship first. A great book that helped me in this area is *The Gift of Asking* by Kemi Nekvapil. In it, Kemi identifies 15 costs of not asking on women (but these also apply more broadly) and these have encouraged me to never fear asking – I am just careful about how I do it. It will be awkward and weird at first, but I truly believe anyone can build a wonderful new yay-bourhood at any time if they are willing.

The right yay-bour for the right situation

I have also come to learn that it's not just building the right network around you, but also harnessing the people in it most effectively. It is likely that you will turn to different people for different specific scenarios in your life. Once you've got your people around you, knowing who to go to and when can also have a hugely positive impact on you.

An example of this for me came when Nic and I moved very quickly from being romantic partners to also being business partners. We went from living very separate lives to working from our shared home in close quarters for long hours, which was quite a challenging transition in the early days. One of the first differences we encountered was our approach to new ideas: as I've said, I'm incredibly bubbly and excitable, while Nic is very solutions-based and practical. Many an argument was had when I would pitch a new idea, totally carried away with how wonderfully it could turn out by 2050, only to have Nic respond with conservative excitement followed by a list of all the practical obstacles we would have to overcome to achieve my dream. Both approaches are important at different phases of conceiving a new idea, but I often felt that Nic was bursting my bubble by identifying problems. I'd feel resentful towards him, meanwhile, he'd feel the same way towards me for dismissing his contributions.

I have since learned to pitch my ideas to a fellow bubbly, over-excitable friend first. They will encourage me to believe it's possible in the abstract, and I only approach Nic once we're ready to tackle the important realities of bringing it to life. Just like every other chapter so far, it's all a matter of knowing what you need, when you need it and structuring your life around that. Side note: if you happen to be in business/work with your husband, then *Men are from Mars, Women are from Venus* by John Gray is a seriously insightful and useful read.

There are many more contrasts between Nic and I that have worked in our favour as a unit, both in business and personally. Again, reinforcing the benefits of having a diverse range of skills and strengths around you (but also knowing when to use them). In my experience of business partnerships, it makes things so much easier when skills and responsibilities don't overlap too much and departments are divvied up accordingly. We have followed this format at Matcha Mylkbar, and this has meant our business and personal relationships with Mark have both continued to thrive.

Our personal life has been much the same, although perhaps not in the way you'd expect. Unlike our approach to micro ideas with bigger macro plans, Nic is the wildly spontaneous, adventure-seeking serial entrepreneur while I've traditionally been the more risk-averse, highly planned, legally trained lover of dot points. This combination has made us invaluable additions to each other's top-five people, cancelling out our more extreme ends of the spectrum and moving us somewhere towards the more balanced middle ground. I have helped bring a little more structure and organisation to Nic's world, channelling his creativity more efficiently and removing a lot of the spontaneity-caused stress from his day-to-day life; Nic has helped relax my formerly very rigid need for pre-planning and predictability, warming me up to the joys of winging it and going on random, spontaneous adventures.

The personal yay-bourhood

Surrounding myself with people who have diverse skills and perspectives has also continued to be a theme in my personal village. I always try to have a good balance of friends who are very like me, as well as those who are different to me in areas that are important for me to be around. The company you keep and those you lean on in pivotal moments of your life can make all the difference as to whether you make things happen or not. As you saw, Jess Hatzis of Frank Body building me up and encouraging our idea for Matcha Maiden rather than knocking it down or criticising it is what quelled my self-doubt in that moment and allowed me to take the next steps.

Similarly, while feeling completely out of my depths during my first podcast recording with the delightful Rachael Finch, her patience and constant reassurance gave me such a boost of confidence and belief that I should continue with the project (for which I am eternally grateful). Had she been disparaging or even disinterested, I might have come away feeling disheartened and deflated about my abilities. When I am racked with such self-doubt or feeling vulnerable for any other reason, I need to be surrounded by friends who share my optimistic, bubbly attitude towards things so I feel heard and understood until I can work through what I'm feeling. I am lucky to have an incredible bunch of fellow excitable friends in my network who are almost like sisters – I turn to them for different things at different times.

One of my dearest friends and the maid of honour at our wedding, Ebony Booth, is so similar to me in the way I think about life that we almost support each other sometimes without needing to say anything at all. We take comfort from just knowing there's someone else who 'gets us'. When I'm brewing new ideas or next steps and need a supportive and open-minded ear, I run things past Eb for a sense check. She'll either jump up and down with excitement or give me honest, constructive criticism in a way that's gentle and still encouraging, and I hope I do the same for her. Same goes with my dear friend, Ruby Morgan – we've lived in different states, continents and time zones across so many chapters of our lives but are always the same no matter how much time passes.

One of our youngest and closest friends, Ang (pro-nounced 'Ange' not like 'bang') Roan, is also very similar to me when it comes to exploring possibilities. She is often the one I celebrate a Matcha Maiden idea with before we dissect it – she calls this 'stomping' over an idea. She's the younger sister of one of my school friends and she came back into my life years later when she started working as an intern for Matcha Maiden while starting her physiotherapy degree. Ang very quickly got absorbed more formally into our Matcha Maiden family. She lives without fear or inhibition with the action-inspiring motto of giving everything a red-hot crack. In both our Matcha Maiden work and personal lives, I often turn to her to stomp over ideas when I need her excitable energy and encouragement.

 Ang is a totally refreshing, unburdened source of energy in our lives and can pull me out of a funk instantly.

On the flip side, however, Ang is different to me in such impactful ways. While I have certainly become more open-minded and less structured than I was in my law days, my natural tendency is back in that direction, and I revert to my childhood drama queen and take life far too seriously. Ang is a totally refreshing, unburdened source of energy in our lives and can pull me out of a funk instantly. While she and I are alike when it comes to celebrating the small things and getting over-excited about new possibilities, she is so different in areas I want to emulate. This keeps the inner child alive in both Nic and me. Anytime we're at risk of starting to feel old and weary as we advance in our thirties, Ang will hit us with a streamer-and-balloon-filled room for our birthday or waltz into a meeting in a carrot costume. And she's at pains to help me with my blooper posts, collecting the ugliest photos of my face that exist and sending them to me whenever I need a good giggle or a pull back down to earth.

Another person who has had an eye-opening and horizon-expanding impact on me is my dear friend, Samantha Gash. Again, we are similar in many ways – namely the ones that first drew our attention to each other. We would obnoxiously answer all the questions in our law lectures, later forming a hardcore two-person study group. But we are also completely different in many ways, namely my conservative, comfort-driven former self and Samantha's thirst for the crazy and impossible. While my extracurricular under-takings at uni involved exchanges to Paris, Samantha volunteered on death row in the United States and made her first moves into the world of ultramarathon running. She was a complete non-runner back then, mind you.

One of her ways to show love for her friends is to push them completely out of their comfort zones, whether they can appreciate the value of that at the time or not. One of the first real camping experiences of my life was in the mountains between Pakistan and Afghanistan, where I joined her support crew for a 220-kilometre ultramarathon between the two highest roads in the world. I attribute so much of my tolerance and even passion for discomfort to Samantha and the influence of her friendship over the years. Coming back to the area of self-doubt, while some friends reassure me with a girly chat or a hug, Samantha reassures me by example.

Samantha continually defies the meaning of impossible by embarking on challenges that have literally never been done before. She can also cut the fluff and tell things to me straight when I need that, too. Watching her walk away from law a few years before me to embark on a career as an elite endurance athlete was a huge influence on me and informed my decision to take the jump. I could give you so many other examples to show that the impact of the people around you is immeasurable; I believe nothing can arm you better or obstruct you more severely. Even for the lone wolves out there, it's so important to look carefully at the people around you and make sure you're happy with how they reflect who you are and where you're going.

Nurture your yay-bourhood

There is a lot of content around about how to build yourself a village or network successfully, but we often skate over how to nurture and maintain it. In this area (as in many), Emma Isaacs is one of the women I look up to most. Her 'softly, softly, gentle approach' to networking reminds me to respect and take care of my relationships. While I'm all for boldly breaking the circle or sending out a cold-call email to approach a new connection, once you've established that relationship it becomes so much more about sustainably building trust and mutual respect. In your existing relationships, too, there are so many small touches and lovely ways you can recognise and thank the people around you who contribute to your way to yay as you progress. Maya Angelou talked about how people remember someone based on how that person made them *feel*, not what they did or said. It's probably not surprising that the feeling I want to leave everyone with is a sense of yay, but also with a sense of the love and appreciation I have for them.

Over the years, what I have noticed and admire is how Emma treats all her relationships equally with patience, discretion and close attention. She even takes the time to regularly handwrite cards on special occasions. My first one turned up with a golden retriever on the front, and how she had the bandwidth to remember the breed of our dog is beyond me. This inspires me to put time and energy into nurturing my own relationships with a similar personalised touch.

Maya Angelou talked about how people remember someone based on how that person made them *feel*, not what they did or said.

With Matcha Maiden, for example, we regularly run reports on our most regular or longest-standing customers and send them out a free bag with a thank you note. And I have long kept a document with significant birthdays to remind myself to organise a flower delivery or gift in advance of the date. If we know someone is going through an illness or a hard time, I love compiling care packages of my favourite things to send their way. There are so many small things you can do to make someone's day and show them you appreciate them.

Someone once advised me to take the time to thank every journalist who ever bothers writing an article about you with a personal card or other form of appreciation for their time, even if you didn't ask for the piece to be written. Ironically, I can't remember who it was that told me this; I wish I could. If it was you, thank you for the excellent advice and please send me your address for the personal card. I still do this every time we are mentioned in press to show our appreciation for someone bothering to write a story. Many times, this gratitude has led to ongoing working relationships for years to come.

When you set out on your way to yay, you're not generally in it for the short term, so it's vitally important to build your relationships with longevity in mind. There will be times when it's easy to get distracted by a shorter-term quick-fix result, but this could be to the detriment of longer-term goals. There may be other times when you want something so badly and can see how beneficial it could be for everybody, but if you're forcing the situation, you could even reduce your chances of success by pushing too hard. Good things take time and meaningful relationships don't blossom overnight. Given the huge impact the people around you have on you, investing patiently and mindfully in those will always pay dividends in the long run.

Justin Dry, co-founder and CEO of trailblazing wine business Vinomofo, wrote an article recently on the impact of spontaneous gifting or gestures of appreciation. Justin is another person I am so grateful to have in the yay-bourhood off the back of one of my 'cold-call' emails. Vinomofo has even introduced a Random Acts of Kindness initiative into their business. After featuring him on the podcast, I was the very lucky recipient of a beautiful bottle of Bellebonne from Justin and his wife, Asher. Since we loved getting to know them over a few chats, Nic and I took Asher and Justin out to a long, leisurely lunch a few weeks later. We gently nurtured our relationship over time and enjoyed each other's company without needing anything from the other.

Much later, when I approached the celebrated marketing maverick Gary Vaynerchuk (aka Gary Vee) to come on my podcast during his whirlwind trip to Australia, I was blown away to receive a very speedy 'yes'. I found out that Justin had partnered with Gary's wine label, Empathy Wines, and had put in a *very* kind word about his experience on my podcast and that had swayed the decision in my favour. Gary's former chief strategy officer, Justine Bloome, was another delightful early guest of the podcast. She also put in a word for me, as I later found out, for which I am eternally grateful. You never know the ways your yay-bourhood might come to support you in the wings.

 Good things take time and meaningful relationships don't blossom overnight.

In situations like this, you might find that you want to nurture your villagers, but don't feel that there is a way you can directly repay someone's kindness or support. I personally find this situation somewhat uncomfortable, but have discovered that you don't always need to return a favour in kind but rather be open to helping out whenever a need arises. Many times, for us, an opportunity will come later down the track to turn the tables. Within a supportive network of people, everything ultimately tends to come out in the wash.

A beautiful dimension to the business community that I've also discovered is that sometimes you never get the opportunity to thank those who have helped you specifically. Instead, you are expected to pay it forward to those who are stepping into your earlier shoes. I have spent many hours mentoring and supporting new business owners to show gratitude for those who did the same for me. I hope that, one day, they will do the same for whoever follows next.

Love your loved ones

Outside of the more professional relationships in your life, your personal relationships are even more prone to being overlooked when life gets busy and stressful. It can be easy to take your loved ones for granted because you know there'll always be there, which is perhaps even more reason why it is important to show your appreciation for those relationships.

It's natural to get snappy, short or plain non-communicative with those around us when we're exhausted or under pressure, but the people closest to you are your lifeblood, so it's always worth taking a deep breath to consider if giving them a hug is a better choice. Nic and I regularly make conscious time for each other that is separate to our working time together: we plan date nights or an adventure and try to never go to sleep angry with each other. I also have regular mother-daughter dates with Mum where we set aside time to watch a movie or go for a massage, just the two of us. If you can't physically be there for your loved ones, even a small text or phone call can help them know you are thinking of them.

Things come in waves. One day, you will need that support back, so always give love and support freely to the ones who love you most. As you've seen, with a lot of our friends, our relationships cross the spectrum between work and personal, making it even more important to nurture those attentively. The times the tables have turned are countless. Such is the nature of long-term friendships that things come back around (provided you are always willing to do your bit without needing something immediately in return).

While I'm at it, even in the case of people you've never met, it is so easy to make somebody else's day and thereby bring some light to your own. A compliment or offer of help costs you nothing but can completely change the course of the day for someone else. My very wise mum always told me to live in such a way that if someone spoke badly of you, nobody would believe it. I try to apply this advice to all my interactions with people, and this is why I spend so much time with her. What a woman!

When Gary Vee joined the podcast, he was at pains to impress upon listeners that the goal isn't necessarily about building businesses and innovating but about the importance of simple kindness. He explained that 'kindness is the ultimate strength, both in business and in life.' One of my favourite quotes from our chat was this: 'Kindness is karma. Give more than you take, and doing the right thing is always the right thing.' Another thing that struck me about Gary – something that I imagine has been hugely impactful in getting him to where he is today – was his humility in the face of his enormous success and celebrity status.

He gave me his complete and unwavering attention for the whole time we spoke. As he wrote in a blog post, 'I think it's incredibly important to know when to turn on your confidence, especially when people push against you, and when people are razzing you, trolling you or doubting you, and I think it's equally important to know when to deploy your humility when people say that "you're the best" or you are a marketing genius or the best business person or anything of that nature.'

In every interaction that you have with anyone in or around your village, I think that striving for that delicate and interesting blend of confidence and humility can benefit you enormously. That doesn't necessarily mean thinking less of yourself, but simply thinking of yourself less. Doing this will allow you to connect deeply with people, learn as much as you can from those around you and see endless possibilities for your relationships and abilities.

CHAPTER 6

Reason, season or lifetime?

One thing I used to lament when I was younger, but have come to understand more over time, is this: as you change through your life, your relationships will as well. While you need to build a supportive and nurturing yay-bourhood around you, it is probably going to change in size and composition many times throughout your life for all sorts of reasons. The first few times you drift out of relationships or lose them altogether can be quite jarring and upsetting, but something my mum taught me (one of her many pearls of wisdom) is that some people are only meant to be in your life for a specific time – the same goes for you in their life. Sometimes, a relationship might highlight ways *you* might not be acting so great and show you what you need to do to grow or change for the better.

There's a phrase my mum always reminds me of, when reflecting on relationships: 'Some come into your life for a reason, some just for a season, and some even for a lifetime.' Once you start to apply this mentality to your friendships and figure out who falls where, change becomes so much easier to navigate and accept. So, while some people who join your village will be a constant throughout your life, others may only be part of a chapter or 'season' along your way to yay and that's absolutely okay. Sometimes the reason someone enters your life isn't necessarily a warm and fuzzy one either. Very often, a person will come along to teach you a valuable lesson that might not feel so great at the time.

This perspective has helped me many times when cherished or long-term friendships haven't turned out to be 'lifers' because we've drifted apart over time or changed in other ways. Similarly, relationships that don't work out or break your heart can be a highly insightful exercise that help you work out the things you need (or don't need) for the next love affair to work well. More importantly, though, Mum's words have helped me navigate those relationships visited upon us in life as ones that we *haven't* necessarily sought out or chosen for our yay-bourhood. While we can carefully curate our innermost village, there will always be people you have to interact with throughout your life through work or in social circles where you don't have as much control or choice in the matter. Bullies or 'psychological vampires', for example, might come into your life to instil in you the strength and resilience you will need later in life for something more important. By focusing on what a relationship, even an unpleasant one, taught you, it can be easier to make sense of it. Every relationship has a role to play, it's for us to decide what that is and how we can learn from it.

The most obvious example of a shift in relationships on my way to yay was the not unpleasant but natural one that followed my complete change of career and lifestyle. Even though I had wonderful relationships with people in the legal profession separate to our working life, my connection with some of them was based primarily on our shared experiences day-to-day. It makes sense that when I moved worlds completely, my village needed to evolve accordingly to reflect that change in season, particularly in terms of my mentors or peers. I needed people to look up to who reflected the different work I would now be doing and to guide me in new areas in which I'd need upskilling. Of course, I'm not suggesting that you should just dump everyone from a former world completely and abruptly to pick up entirely new connections (although for some people, this might be a healthy evolution. I'm simply saying to let relationships shift and evolve as things around you start to change.

For some people, this evolution happens when they move countries or cities and need to form a new village for themselves in their new locale. Any major shift like parenthood, illness or the many other vicissitudes of life that affects your priorities, needs and activity, is probably going to require some moulding of the yay-bourhood. I think many of us spend a lot of time lamenting or worrying about those changes, but coming back to the reason/season/lifetime mentality has always helped me get perspective. Just like we will go through many different chapters in our way to yay, so too will the people we need and are needed by on that journey.

You can't live a positive life in a negative environment

A more pressing example in the context of seizing your yay is not necessarily these natural evolutions in a village, but rather the occasions that warrant a bit of active 'culling' of its members. So far, we've been focusing on the wonderful ways people can add depth and value to your journey, and how the support of others can get you over the line when you need that extra push. But, equally, the opposite can often be the case, and people can be the big fat nay in your way to yay. For some of you, the sceptics in your network who are unable to believe in your ability to achieve things outside their realm of understanding may be knocking your ideas down as a result. For others, there may be outright haters in your life who are jealous or resentful of your success. There might also be family members or close friends who aren't 'against' you, but whose belief or value systems mean they don't necessarily value the industry you want to move into.

 There may be outright haters in your village who are jealous or resentful of your success.

While we had incredible support from family and friends when first starting Matcha Maiden and Matcha Mylkbar, there were equally people around us who thought I was crazy to leave a respectable, stable career in favour of an 'Instagram business'. While I didn't face the strong or aggressive opposition that many people have experienced when making a drastic life change, I did face some vocal scepticism and bewilderment in a way that often triggered me to start doubting or overthinking my decision. In most cases, it wasn't coming from a negative place at all, but rather a position of concern for my welfare and a desire to warn me against doing something rash or silly. In some cases, however, it did seem the barrage of 'special comments' was based on resentment or envy, especially where the person was unhappy in their own lives and unable or unwilling to make a change themselves. Either way, I found in those early days of the transition that I needed to distance myself from those voices until I was resolute enough myself to withstand their questioning or doubts. I've always found it so funny how easily we judge and make comments on others as if our opinions are imperative to their lives.

Unfortunately, there will always be people in your circle who aren't necessarily as on board with your dreams as you are, so it's so important to build your network so that those individuals can't negatively impact your mindset or actions. My best advice is not to waste energy trying to change their minds but rather to change the way you manage their comments or opinions internally. There is so much in life that we have no control over, including the decisions others make about the way they behave in relation to you, but there is equally so much we can control about how we let those things affect us and that's where our energy should be focused. Hateful or negative interactions will naturally always deliver a sting, but, just like with self-doubt, the most important thing is to acknowledge the feeling but learn how *not* to let it go any further or change any of your actions as a response.

Of course, tuning out negativity is easier said than done but I've found a few sayings or principles that help ground me and keep my thoughts on track. There are so many variations on these mantras that I turn to in this area, but I'll share four of my favourites:

1. **If haters bring you down, it only means they are beneath you; every time someone criticises or judges you, it reflects something going on with them and not with you. I'm sure many of you can think of a time where someone has questioned or criticised something you're doing not because they wouldn't love to be in your position, but because they *aren't* or can't be and resent that.**

2. **If you're doing something that bothers someone enough to spend time and energy on hating rather than on their own stuff, it just means you're doing something big enough to elicit that. Basically, it's a sign you've made it! I remember the first time we received a negative review for Matcha Maiden that was unduly harsh and levelled at us and our authenticity personally, and I was absolutely devastated. A good friend and mentor wisely reminded me that the only way to avoid displeasing people is to stand for nothing or do nothing different at all.**

3. Even if someone isn't necessarily a 'hater' but simply isn't supportive of what you're doing, you should never let this dull your sparkle simply because it's shining in their eyes. Often, people withhold support because you're defying the limits of what they believe is possible, but it's not on you to drop back to their level to bring them comfort. I found this among some of my legal colleagues who definitely weren't nasty or unpleasant at all, but who felt challenged by how well things had gone after I walked away from law and how much fun I seemed to be having while still making a living. They'd avoid asking me or talking about the business at all and, if I was asked, I often found myself playing down how well things were going or what a great time I was having to make it easier. Especially with colleagues with whom I had bonded over complaining about the long hours and lack of freedom, I found it hard to rub it in their faces that I was living such an exciting life with so much control over my time. But I have learned that self-editing for others is not the best strategy and strips you of your joy.

4. (And this one's my favourite.) Don't let anyone rent a space in your head unless they're a good tenant. Like our energy and time, our headspace is finite and there are already too many important things competing up there for space to let something unworthy sneak in and wreak havoc. I've definitely been guilty of letting someone's words or

behaviour plague my mind for hours or days, before realising that doesn't affect anyone but me (and especially not them). If you're going to let anyone creep into your thoughts, make sure they're making a happy, uplifting contribution to that precious space of yours or kick them right out.

Sometimes, putting ideas into a practical analogy makes the message much clearer – like that fourth principle. Just as you wouldn't tolerate a tenant who trashed your place and spread negativity, you shouldn't tolerate a tenant in your mind who does the same. We are all running our own race and the people who don't respect you and your race are simply not your people. While I still sometimes want to be everybody's person, I've been much happier since I've realised nobody is meant to be, and that's okay.

The beauty of building boundaries

While I absolutely loved letting go of any type of boundary when I first left the corporate world, I have come back to appreciating that *some* boundaries are necessary and important in most areas of our life. In the case of curating a positive network around us that will best serve our happiness and success while also limiting any potential negative impact those relationships could have, boundaries can be our strongest tool.

Like many things, this is easier said than done. I still sometimes find myself spiralling in response to negative comments from outsiders or letting other kinds of unpleasant interactions further into my psyche than I should. My podcast, for example, has had overwhelmingly delightful feedback, but a single reviewer recently asked 'if the host would stop loving her voice so much and shut up for a moment'. This toppled me. Even though it was just one comment among thousands of positive ones, I found myself recoiling in worry and angst for days.

The trick is to learn how to get yourself back on track as soon as you can and find ways to address that negative influence in a way that allows you to avoid it again or limit its impact in the future. I come back to the concept of metacognition and thinking about my own thoughts. I try to observe the negative response I'm having, rationally accept where it has come from, but then consciously push it away before it snowballs into something bigger. Depending on the relationship or situation, putting up some healthy boundaries for next time could be anything from a complete walk away from the relationship to a gentler way of introducing some distance with that person. It took me a very long time to accept that I didn't need to be friends with everyone forever. Once I understood this, everything started to flourish.

If you're struggling with relationships that are actively toxic in your life (I'm sure we've all experienced at least one, if not several), something I've learned is that you don't always need to salvage them. It's okay to let those relationships go. These toxic relationships might be old friendships you thought would last a lifetime, but instead your friend has become resentful and sour as you progress. They can be newer friendships that have become toxic or sabotaging for one reason or another. Usually, you can extract a lesson or a 'reason' for that person coming into your life. Whatever it may be, a quote that I love in this situation to remind me to stop trying to change myself to please everyone is that, 'When a flower doesn't bloom, you fix the environment in which it grows, not the flower.'

Similarly, toxic relationships can form online, too, even if you don't know the person. This is especially true in the case of online haters who troll people on social media. While it is often tempting to fight back and engage with a troll, sometimes, the most powerful way you can confront their negativity is to block them from your feed altogether. Many of my podcast guests are people in the public eye who have faced haters in a serious way. Rachael Finch's top tip for avoiding online bullies is to completely ignore them rather than indulge their negative attacks with a response. This is kind of like the blinkering strategy we talked about in chapter 4 in relation to social comparison; this same strategy can be effective with any real-world relationships that leave you feeling threatened, highly anxious or crappy about yourself.

As someone who's spent some time, thankfully not too much, fielding messages from online trolls, I've spent many hours agonising over why anyone would want to spend their life sabotaging another person's success. There can be many reasons for why other people act in the ways they do, but many times it actually has nothing to do with you at all; it's about what's going on with them. I know some people really don't like hearing that having haters is a compliment because it means you are doing well but, many times, it genuinely is (in a backwards kind of way).

The trick is to put things back in a 'yay frame'. The simple fact of life is that you can't be everyone's kind of person – it's inevitable that you are going to rub some of the billions of people on Earth the wrong way. Admittedly, this is something my internal people-pleaser is still coming to terms with; it doesn't sit well with me that I can't be liked by everyone. But it doesn't matter what's going on in the other person's world; the only thing that *really* matters is how you react to them and what you do to limit the negative consequences their words or actions have on you.

People have, of course, behaved unpleasantly towards me in some way or another on my way to yay. It's important to remember that taking *reasonable* criticism on board and using it as a prompt to improve ourselves is important for growth, but there have definitely been times where the criticism directed at me has crossed the line from constructive or reasonable feedback. I've had my authenticity and values as a businessperson attacked and seen this message spread to others in our community. I've had very personal intrusions into my life with Nic – people claiming all kinds of things or injecting toxic waves into our relationships just for the fun of it. I've also experienced situations that forced me to confront my inability to please everyone or be everyone's best friend. All of these, however, have helped me develop resilience, patience, empathy and understanding.

I won't pretend these experiences didn't cause me to launch into a downward spiral. Naturally, I questioned myself, my stomach clenched with anxiety and I rehashed those moments incessantly to the detriment of all my actual priorities in life. But, in most cases, these moments taught me something valuable for the long run. When I look back on these attacks, they still sting and feel like a shock to the system – after all, we're not expected to love or welcome these situations into our life. But we can expect to act in ways and implement boundaries that limit the negative impact they can have on our mindset and energy. And, with that in mind . . .

The clean-out cull

The process of culling (metaphorically speaking, of course) those people in your life who try to sabotage you or make you feel crappy will look different for each person *and* each relationship. It can feel awkward, difficult and messy to extract a toxic person from your circle, but that doesn't mean it's not the right thing for you. Sometimes, there's a bit of a risk of things blowing up into a fight or it can be a lengthy, painful process to make others accept and respect your boundaries. In other cases, you might not need to actively 'do' anything at all. Making an internal, emotional decision to distance yourself from the behaviours of that person might be enough. There are many ways culling can play out, depending on the situation:

- a clear, upfront discussion in person about how you feel;
- the softer 'phase out' mentioned above; or
- an all-out walking away and separation to cut that person from your life.

If you feel comfortable with a clear, upfront discussion, as many of you will, that's always a good way to approach matters in relationships. For better or worse, confrontation is not one of my biggest strengths (to the point where even writing about it here is making me uncomfortable), so if you're like me you may prefer the gentler 'phase out' approach; you don't owe anyone who is playing a toxic role in your life an explanation.

There may be people in your life who aren't actively toxic or sabotaging you but who just aren't supportive of what you're doing. These might be the situations where you simply distance yourself *temporarily* while you're building your dream – whatever that may be, like I did when my corporate friends' scepticism or worry was proving challenging to my confidence and focus. Sometimes you need certain people in your life for certain situations, and those people may just not be your 'hustle' people, which is absolutely fine – you've already seen how important it is to make sure you *do* turn to the right people in the pivotal moment of making a big, scary decision. Reserve these friendships, instead, for the things you do share or enjoy together, and quarantine the parts of your life you have other people for. I have friends in my life who I barely speak to about business because that's just not the common ground our friendship is based on. It all comes back, again, to setting up the right boundaries for your life wherever you need them most, and then sticking to them.

Family naysayers

One of the most difficult and probably most painful situations to tackle is when the negative influence is a member of your family or a person who you can't necessarily move on from easily. When I walked away from a sensible, academically focused career, I didn't have to sidestep any 'tiger parents' (being adopted) but I know many friends leaving their jobs for business did. So, fortunately for me, I don't have any real-life experience of negativity in this area – my family has only ever been fully supportive of the choices we make. They trust that Nic and I consider all the options carefully and that we would cope and learn our lesson if things fail). While my parents did go through a challenging separation, the resulting distance between certain family members was more gradual than an act of putting up barriers. So, I'm not speaking from experience here and understand the best strategy would depend on the unique complexities and nature of each particular family situation.

From the experience of friends, though, and extrapolating from other relationships, I would suggest that if you can't physically create the distance you need from someone in your family, perhaps you can internally create mental barriers. This can be helpful in family situations where you can't physically remove yourself in the same way you can from a toxic boss at work. Perhaps you could decide that career is a topic of conversation that you turn to friends or others outside of your family with, instead of bringing it up in a context you know will become heated. Alternatively, you could build a place in your mind to retreat to, which helps you endure the conversations or family environments that otherwise induce stress. Arianna Huffington's sister, Agapi Stassinopoulos, describes a practical technique called the 'portable paradise' in her book *Wake Up to the Joy of You* that involves building and solidifying your inner tranquil environment so the external environment can't pull you down. You can also seek external or professional help to navigate the complexity of the situation, which those close to me have had great success with.

When challenges come from family or otherwise, I often find it hard not to wonder why people aren't all on the same page as I am, or why all relationships don't just work out between well-intentioned people. As Rodney King said in what has since become a viral meme, 'Can we all get along?' But I realise increasingly that with as many different personalities and backgrounds as the world holds, of course we can't all be compatible with everybody. It is for us, simply, to find those we are compatible with and learn to manage everyone else as best we can.

Clear, concise communication

Having gone through all the situations that warrant distance, sometimes the challenges we face within our relationships are just a matter of figuring out your communication styles. One of the most impactful books I have ever read (I've gifted many of my friends and family copies), is a book by Gary Chapman called *The Five Love Languages*. It is based on the idea that we all show and receive love in different ways. This is how I think of them:

1. Words of affirmation: saying kind or supportive things and vocalising the way we feel about people or things for their benefit.
2. Acts of service: showing how we feel through our behaviours or gestures towards others, like making a meal for someone or helping them with a task.
3. Giving or receiving gifts: this one's self-explanatory. A physical and symbolic way to show care.
4. Quality time: setting aside time to be present and give someone your full attention.
5. Physical touch: hugs, massages, cuddles, kisses, etc.

We all adopt a mix of each of these in the way we care for others, and we respond best to a mix of each of them in how others treat us. Some of these styles will be more dominant than others, and, most importantly, they will not necessarily match (or be compatible with your partner's). Breakdowns of communication that feel like breakdowns in a relationship can simply be the result of not understanding the way each other is trying to show care. This goes for relationships in the business world, too, where love doesn't come into the equation, but the styles of communication are still actively in play.

This is one of the few books that changed my entire perspective on something that permeates my whole life. It has helped me understand my loved ones and our relationships (as well as, more broadly, our many relationships in business) so much better, and also reminds me that we all express ourselves differently. Nic offering me reasons why I can't do something or the many ways an idea of mine needs to be fixed *isn't* actually him trying to be a buzzkill, it's his way of showing he cares enough about my idea to help me overcome the practical obstacles before I begin. My friend Samantha has a very blunt way of asking provocative questions about my life that used to put me off-balance. Now, I now understand that this is her way of showing she cares about helping me explore different aspects of things.

One of my favourite ways to show love for my friends is to give (or more often, make) very personalised, thoughtful gifts that relate to specific shared experiences or things that are very unique to that person. However, my preferred expression of receiving love is *not* receiving gifts, I much prefer words of affirmation (long cards or lovely messages) and acts of service (people showing their appreciation or love through gestures and actions).

Whether you subscribe to these five love languages or not, the important message here is that we all show our feelings differently. Inevitably, there will be people you are so entirely incompatible with that you just can't find mutual ground. And, on this note, there are a couple more things worth mentioning that have really helped me in my harder interactions with people, both personally and professionally. Time to break out my beloved dot points.

- When things don't work out particularly well with someone, especially if they are at fault, **learn to let it go quickly** so you can move on with your yay. According to the famous Buddhist proverb, 'Holding a grudge is like drinking poison and expecting the other person to die.' We tend to hold onto things when we are wronged or upset, and we let them fester in our heads – building negativity. Sometimes, without realising it, a person or situation can take up valuable space in your mind and drain energy away from your true goals. The only person you are hurting in that situation is yourself because the other person is entirely unaffected by your internal grudge and resentment. Forgiving someone is powerful not because it means what they did is okay, but because it liberates *you* from being stuck.

- **When someone says no to you, don't take it as a universal no.** It simply means you can't do it right now or that you can't do it *with them*, and there will be someone else out there who will say yes. Again, it's too easy to let one small situation build up to feel all-encompassing and affect our decisions accordingly. Learning to cope with rejection, big or small, is one of the most valuable skills you can develop because you become resilient. It is so important not to confuse someone's rejection of your idea or request with a commentary on your personal value or the value of your idea. A 'no' is generally a reflection of their circumstances at that moment or their *unique* opinion, and not everyone's. Develop the ability to bounce back as quickly as you can so you can find that person out there who *is* the right one for you and your idea.

- Contrary to what my legal brain might once have told me, **you don't have to attend every argument you're invited to.** (It's hard, though, because I do feel like I'm so good at winning them.) Silence is as powerful a response as any, and it can nip a disagreement in the bud before it snowballs into anything more serious and burdensome. Some people are argumentative and will take up your time and energy with their opinions unless you put up the walls and stop them in their tracks. Even if you *are* right, always ask yourself if it's worth giving up your peace to prove that.

- **Don't make permanent decisions based on temporary feelings.** Many people can be too quick to react in the heat of the moment when it comes to certain situations or people, but we must always be careful not to let passing feelings have long-term consequences for us. Something I've been doing for many years, again at Mum's encouragement, is writing phantom responses to people when I need to act in a heated moment. I've got a very long fuse so you'll rarely find me angry, but, of course, on occasion I can get triggered by all sorts of things. Though less so now than when I was younger. I find it so cathartic to open a blank email or text and power out the response I'd like to send or text. I go to town, saying everything I'd say if I let my emotions get the better of me, but I leave the recipient space blank. That way, I won't accidentally press send. Once I'm done, I sit on that draft until I've calmed down and seen reason. Later, I'll come back to it and either give it a more level-headed edit or scrap it altogether. By then, most of my emotions have passed. I've got them out of my system, and I haven't risked saying anything silly or hurtful and suffering the consequences.
- **Do what is right, not what is easy.** As Gary Vee told me, 'Doing the right thing is always the right thing.' Brené Brown

often says (and Kemi Nekvapil always reminds me) that 'Clear is kind'. Sometimes, hard conversations need to be had and being honest is the best and kindest way you can serve someone. Another way I like saying this is that we should say what we *think*, not what we think we *should* say. I find conversations absolutely excruciating if they involve any sort of confrontation, but I know that these are the times I need to push through, because it's the right thing to do. Same goes for actions: sometimes we need to do things that are uncomfortable or challenging because they are the most ethical way forward. Shortcuts will never get you where you want to end up in the long run.

- Finally, and this is one I absolutely love but need constant reminding of: **if it costs you your peace, it's too expensive.** I love the way this expression reframes peace and happiness or equilibrium as a currency that we can choose to spend rather than a state of being that we slip into helplessly and have no control over. I've let so many things bother me for much longer than they've deserved simply because I've chosen not to interrupt them in their tracks. Our time is precious and finite, and every minute that something makes us unsettled or unhappy is actively stealing a minute of happiness from us. If something is going to cause you drama or bother you, it's generally not worth your time. Life is too short and beautiful to be wasted on things that don't bring you yay.

When you sit and deeply reflect on how different we are and how differently we all express ourselves, it's a miracle that any of us can get along at all. Relationships can simultaneously be the most energy-consuming, complicated and stressful parts of our lives as well as the most fulfilling, rewarding and nurturing. When you put this down on paper, it all starts to seem a little overwhelming, but I believe most of us have an internal barometer of what's right and what isn't. The important thing is that, like everything else in this book, the choices we make aren't made by default; we are building and nurturing the relationships that provide support, love and yay in both directions.

CHAPTER 7

Yay is a staircase, not an elevator

You've built and moulded your village, and they are helping you shed the self-doubt and bypass comparison. You're ready to set off on your perfectly imperfect way to yay. You may have picked up this book because you've already had your light-bulb moment and been struck by your burning passion or idea, or you may have picked it up because you want to start seizing your yay, but don't yet know what that looks like. My natural tendency is to race to the end to find out what happens and get it all over and done with. I want to find what makes me yay, focus everything on that and live happily ever after. I like to know how things are going to turn out before I get started so I can map everything out and orientate myself in the chronology of my adventure.

Unfortunately, that tends not to be how things go in life, nor in your journey to seizing your yay. Fortunately, however, even if things don't work out how you expect them to, they often work out better.

 You may have picked up this book because you've already had your light-bulb moment and been struck by your burning passion or idea, or you may have picked it up because you want to start seizing your yay, but don't yet know what that looks like.

Thanks to the incredibly interesting and diverse stories I've heard through interviewing guests for my podcast, I've learned that people encounter so many diversions and unexpected steps in their journeys to their goals. Those diversions are ultimately what get them to the top of their staircase, even if that staircase isn't the one they initially set out to climb. We are often introduced to people's stories after they've figured it all out, so it's harder to imagine them losing direction or momentum along the way. However, many of the people you might view as being an overnight success have instead been many tumultuous years in the making, with countless iterations, detours and stops along the way.

At this point, I'd like to take a minute to distinguish between direction and speed. With the glorification of busy and the constant pressure in our society to achieve and progress, we're always in a rush to get to the next best thing. And sometimes, we get so distracted with keeping up our pace that we lose sight of our direction altogether. I often think of my past self as a little hamster running furiously on a wheel, clocking up lots of miles but not necessarily getting any closer to anywhere worth going.

'Busy' does not necessarily mean productive, nor does it have a direction unless you guide it in one. What's more important is to find your direction first, and it's okay if you move towards that slowly, step by step, even if you don't know what's going to come next. Seizing your yay is an act of patience and open-mindedness. When I was a lawyer, I remember stressing endlessly about climbing the corporate ladder and smashing through goals without ever stopping to ask myself if I really cared about them. I realise now that my legal career wasn't the ladder I was supposed to climb, but simply the first of many steps towards the 'me' that I have become. It provided a formidable basis for the career I now have, even though it didn't end up being my forever job.

A way I like to describe my law years is that, without knowing it, I was simply biding my time until the great 'reveYAYtion' of 2014. At the time, I didn't feel like I had any direction, but, with hindsight, I can see what a crucial step those years were: teaching me so many lessons and skills I'd need for what came next. Almost everyone I have interviewed on the podcast (or spoken to in life generally) has been in the position you are in at some point or another and it is a necessary feeling in order to spark the kind of questioning and self-investigation that leads to a fulfilling and yay-driven life. Very few among us know, with conviction, what path we are destined for when we first choose our careers, although rare exceptions do exist. What I want to impress on you here is that the point isn't just to stumble on your yay one day and then you're done, ready to live out the rest of your days that way. Yay is a journey, not a destination, filled with many steps and twists along the way that must be experienced and worked through to get you to where you're meant to be.

I probably knew quite early on that my legal career didn't light my fire and that it wasn't something I would likely stay in for the long term. As you've learned, I've always been equal parts uber nerd and creative dreamer, so while the academically inclined part of my brain thoroughly enjoyed my work as a lawyer, my creative tendencies were getting no love. The problem was, however, that I didn't necessarily know what alternative *would* best unite those two parts of me – or if such a job even existed. Consequently, I ended up feeling disheartened and directionless.

The reality is that there are bills to pay and life costs

money, so in most cases, we do need to have a job, even if our work doesn't ignite that fiery passion within us. Looking back now, I can see that I was simply too green and young anyway to have started the business that we ended up starting years later. I wasn't yet mature enough to be able to make it succeed in the way we have been able to now – I needed time to learn about the world, to grow into myself and to get used to making adult decisions with real-life consequences. Hence, I truly was just biding my time until the circumstances were right to take the next step towards my yay.

You don't have to see the whole staircase to take the first step

The important thing I take away from that time in my life is that every part of your life is a stepping stone or a step up your staircase to yay, even if it doesn't necessarily feel that way at the time. If you can learn to reframe every part of your life that way and make the absolute best of that situation while you're in it, you might find that this helps you to deal with feeling directionless. You may also start to be able to make more sense of where you are.

I attended my first entrepreneurial event when I was still at university (see, I was taking a small step many years before I knew about the business staircase I'd end up climbing). My friend Samantha Gash was a guest speaker at the very first League of Extraordinary Women event, so I went along to support her. Even though I hadn't even started full-time work I had a vague inkling that I might want to go into business one day. I figured I'd continue attending these kinds of events to keep my mind as open as possible. I enjoyed the event so much that I went to the next one a few months later.

The speaker was Kate Morris of Adore Beauty (another hugely successful business started in a humble garage). I remember it as clear as day: it was a breakfast event and I was so impressed and inspired by Kate that I rushed up to be the first in the queue after she spoke (such a keen bean) and told her how I hadn't even graduated yet but wasn't sure I was going into a career I'd want to end up in. I never dreamed that I would get to speak alongside her years later and laugh about the roller-coaster life of an entrepreneur. Nor did I understand that the many years of attending these events before I knew why I was doing it was, in fact, laying wonderful groundwork for what would come next.

As I now like to remind myself, baby steps still move you forward. These baby steps moved Adore Beauty forward, too – many times without Kate realising where they would lead. Though her way to yay involves less discrete stepping stones between jobs or whole careers than others, there have still been many times within her business where the next step wasn't immediately clear. She's been in business for over 20 years, and has an absolute wealth of knowledge.

To give you some background, Adore Beauty's story starts in a way that Kate describes as 'pretty lo-fi'; like pretty much every other story we've covered so far, which should be infinitely reassuring. She got her start in beauty working a part-time job on the Clarins counter in a department store, and she founded her business at the age of twenty-one. While working at that Clarins counter, she'd noticed that women didn't seem enthralled with the department store shopping experience. She thought that online shopping could be a much more empowering way of shopping. So, despite there being no online beauty sites at the time, Kate borrowed A$12,000 from then-boyfriend now-partner's parents to create the website and buy some stock. As foreign as it may sound now, there were many times when Kate would have to crawl under her desk to unplug the telephone so she could use the internet – and yet she managed to build the first beauty e-commerce site Australia had seen.

There was an endless slew of rejections and many sceptics when she first started but Adore Beauty has continued to thrive over its 20 years in business while many others have bowed out – struggling to adapt to ever-changing times.

That original garage office has been replaced by a warehouse and office with about 150 staff, and 2 million customers visit the website every month (including me). The figures have been extraordinary, seeing a six-fold expansion over the past four years, and at the time of writing this is forecasted to rise to over A$100 million in 2020. Even more impressive given the alarming rate of change in the beauty industry over the past 20 days, let alone the past 20 years.

Given this astronomical expansion, you can see how hard it would have been for Kate to know what the next stepping stone in her journey might be. She relies on her superpowers of brushing off rejection and getting stuff done to consistently push ahead. Adore Beauty has recently announced its expansion in Australia and overseas with an investment from private equity firm Quadrant, so I can only imagine what else the future holds. I'm sure Kate never imagined this might lie somewhere along her staircase.

In my case, since I fully appreciated that I had no idea what I would do if I wasn't a lawyer, I decided the best way to pass the time working at the law firm was to simply learn absolutely everything I could from the situation I was in. I signed up for every possible extracurricular activity and event, including Chinese language classes and corporate triathlons (very watered-down versions of real triathlons, mind you). I did this to interact with as many different people as I could, and to really find out what I enjoyed and what I didn't. I arranged coffee catch-ups with former uni friends or colleagues who were doing different things with their law degree – pro bono work, going in-house at companies rather than law firms, moving into diplomacy or working at firms overseas – to find out more about their pathways. I also tried to learn as much as I possibly could from the people around me, trusting that at least parts of it would always be useful, even if only to show me that's *not* where I wanted to go next.

While I reached out to many connections I already had, I also got a little overzealous and started setting up coffees with clients I'd never actually met – the ones I knew had also started out at law firms. I'd chat to them about potential career pathways and find out how they had ended up where they were. One such client was Neil McCann from ANZ bank. I can't recall the exact details of the file we'd worked on together, but we had exchanged some emails, so when I asked him to meet me for a coffee to pick his brain, he very graciously agreed. I was asking about this long before I really knew why I was asking, but it turned out to be worth doing. It was Neil who a little while later introduced me to Adam Schwab, who became a wonderful mentor for us in business. Adam is in the start-up world and has not only been an invaluable source of guidance and a friend, he has also connected me with many others who have helped us along the way.

The most important thing I remind myself now is that no situation is ever a waste of time unless you let it become that. Even if you don't want to stay where you are forever, there is always something you can learn or some way you can grow yourself that will be useful in your next chapter, whatever that may be. It could be acquiring more skills and taking advantage of training resources if you're working in a big company, or even more broadly, simply investing time in networking and building relationships before you know what you'll need them for. If you don't know where you want to end up, it's going to take you some time to figure that out. But time is going to pass anyway, so you might as well spend it as usefully as you can.

You don't have to like each step

If you're in a job or a phase of your life that you find you don't like, take comfort from the fact that it is a wonderful thing because it shows you where you *don't* want to be. There's always a bright side if you look hard enough at a situation, even if the situation isn't enjoyable at the time you're going through it. Finding out that a pathway isn't for you puts you one step ahead of those people who are still entirely neutral towards their options. You have one more piece of the yay-based puzzle to redirect your next step.

I often say during keynotes or on the podcast that people will be encouraged to make a change in their life when they are actively unhappy or negatively impacted, but rarely will any action be instigated when they're simply indifferent or feeling 'blah' towards a situation. That's what scares me the most looking back now is that I *wasn't* actually actively unhappy with my life as a lawyer at the time. If it weren't for the happy accident that birthed Matcha Maiden, I would never have been exposed to the ways I *could* be better ignited and the entire other world of possibilities that were open to me. This is why I am now so passionate about encouraging you to actively investigate your strengths, weaknesses and passions and take control over your pathyay rather than just accepting what feels okay and never knowing how much better it could have been.

 There's always a bright side if you look hard enough at a situation.

Having said that, I have many friends who have found the perfect balance in nine-to-five jobs they're not necessarily passionate about or feel a little 'blah' towards, but which allow them to pay for the joyous life they live outside of work and that is their pathyay. Sticking with a situation you don't love (or don't feel much about either way) is absolutely fine provided it is a choice you are making in order to find your joy elsewhere, rather than a situation you end up in for lack of considering any other options. Importantly, having a seize the yay philosophy definitely doesn't mean that you have to find yay within your work, even though I was lucky enough to do so myself. It's only recently that we've adopted the assumption that work always has to be enjoyable and fulfilling but historically it's called 'work' for a reason. Your yay might *necessarily* exist outside of your work and lie more in your hobbies or voluntary activities, such as in the case of artists or creatives who find their buzz killed when they have to create to a professional brief or strict schedules. I also want to reiterate that leaving my job to start a business was what brought me fulfillment but that won't necessarily be true for others.

I even have some friends who reversed earlier decisions about starting businesses to step back towards their yay, returning to their former positions of employment after finding that the peripheral parts of running a business distracted them from using their talents and stripped them of their joy. Many of them have, instead, chosen to embrace a more intrapreneurial mindset focusing on creating, innovating and building their business within their employment structure. The important thing is that they tried other things to make that decision *consciously* rather than ending up there by default. Whether it be within or outside your work, in business or in leisure, yay can come from anywhere so long as you are looking for it to begin with.

An example I love to share of the many forms that seizing your yay can take is the case of a delightful woman I interviewed for the podcast, Michelle Birkett, a senior zookeeper at Adelaide Zoo. Michelle always knew what she wanted to do and now she wakes up to her dream job every day. She reminded me that yay doesn't have to involve an insatiable ambition to keep climbing the ladder or moving forwards for the sake of it. She has simply jumped off the forward-pushing hamster wheel altogether and no longer succumbs to society's need for perpetual forward movement. She has found a job that makes her yay every single day, and I was fascinated to hear that she isn't setting her sights on climbing the ladder within the zoo hierarchy and doesn't see herself as ambitious in that way. Progressing up the ladder would, in fact, change her role in a way that would detract from why she loves it so much, and it would mean much more administrative and oversight work, taking her away from hands-on time with the animals.

Your yay might *necessarily* exist outside of your work and lie more in your hobbies or voluntary activities.

Instead, her ambition is focused on doing the job she does have as best she can, to give the animals under her care the best life possible and to always keep learning how to do it better. It was quite new for me to encounter someone who didn't feel pulled to take any other stepping stones and in fact resists those because she knows they would change her role dramatically. I loved finding someone who was absolutely content with where they already were – how delightful to know those people are around. Above all, yay isn't something that takes one particular form. My ultimate goal is just to encourage you all to find it in some form or another that brings depth and fulfilment to your life rather than just an existence.

Not all steps will make sense at the time

Given that most of us probably haven't quite reached zoo-keeper Michelle's kind of yay (based on you picking up this book), let's assume you are still dealing with some stepping stones. As well as not needing to be thrilled with each one, I've found that they also don't necessarily have to make immediate sense at the time to be a step in the right direction. The more experimenting you do with different structures and options in your life, the more you will discover about your likes, dislikes and what fulfils you. This will then lead you to your next part of the staircase.

When we let the need for speed and 'busy' creep back in, we often feel like these diversions and experiments are a waste of time because we need to do everything as quickly as we possibly can and rush to the end. However, there are so many examples of people who have only really stumbled upon their passions much later in their lives, proving that, sometimes, the preliminary stepping stones are lengthy (and often unrelated to your ultimate yay) but totally worthy passages of time. The visionary Vera Wang didn't start designing clothes until she was thirty-nine, Clint Eastwood directed his first film at forty-one, and IBM was started by a sixty-one-year-old. Closer to home, an example of late career blooming I absolutely love to share is that of Nic's former training partner and our dear friend, Jana Pittman.

You may have heard of Jana through her incredible international hurdling career. She fell in love with athletics at the tender age of nine, and is a two-time world champion in the 400-metre hurdles as well as a gold medallist at the 2002 and 2006 Commonwealth Games (and the 4 × 400-metre relay in both). She competed in her first Olympic Games in Sydney at just seventeen years old and was the favourite for her event when the 2004 Athens Olympics came around, but torn cartilage in her right knee meant she couldn't compete. And a week before the 2012 London Olympics, she underwent surgery and still finished up by placing fifth in the final.

At that point, Jana changed sports completely, and ended up competing in the two-woman bobsleigh event at the 2014 Winter Olympics in Sochi, making her the first Australian female athlete to compete in both the Summer and Winter Olympic Games. It would be easy to assume Jana's many athletic achievements comprise her whole way to yay, but what comes next is my favourite part. Jana considers her sporting career to be the warm-up for the new, and entirely unrelated, career chapter she has recently embarked on. While training for the Sochi Winter Olympics in 2013, Jana began a Bachelor of Medicine and Bachelor of Surgery (MBBS), which she has since completed.

Following many years of blood, sweat and tears studying, raising her three beautiful children, competing, speaking all over the country, writing her book *Just Another Hurdle* and everything in between, Jana has officially become a doctor, hoping to move into obstetrics and gynaecology. Fertility is a cause close to Jana's heart with two of her three children being conceived through IVF. She is such a fabulous example of how drastic your diversions along the way to yay can be –

as big as an entire international athletics career that most would consider more than enough for one lifetime. Just because you're on a different pathway to the one you end up on, it doesn't mean you're lost and it doesn't mean you can't find a new one along the way.

As we touched on earlier, so many people we have spoken about also have huge phases of their life before or in the middle of the journey we now know is their pathyay. Lisa Messenger had been running other businesses for *11 years* before she started the Collective Hub empire with all its various offshoots. Other examples include Hugh Jackman, who was a PE teacher at Uppingham School and a party clown before his stellar acting and stage career. Jeff Bezos, best known as the founder, CEO and president of the ever-growing Amazon, had a lucrative career in computer science on Wall Street until he founded Amazon at thirty-one years old. And Sara Blakely, the billionaire founder of revolutionary underwear brand, Spanx, was a door-to-door office supplies saleswoman for seven years in her twenties before launching her business in 2000.

There are many more fun examples of diversionary stepping stones on the way to yay, and some of the best are the phases that ended when people got *fired*. Kate Morris was fired from two of her earlier jobs at a national retailer *and* from an independent pharmacist, and then there's the great Oprah Winfrey, who was fired when she was an evening news reporter (who fires Oprah?!).

Another way your yay might surprise you is by manifesting in a different form than you expected. As you know, mine came after a stint in Hong Kong, but I had, in fact, decided to *stop* trying to find my purpose at that time. I'd decided to just enjoy the beautiful experience of living in a different country, entirely unburdened by the obligations and responsibilities back home. Side note: if you get the chance to do an expat stint, do it! I can't recommend it enough.

Another great friend of ours, Michael Ramsey, started out in marketing for the oil and gas industry. He also had a boating technology start-up on the side that he launched with his dad. Michael ended up seizing his yay in a completely different industry after getting his personal training qualifications on the side, which ultimately led him to build an incredible health and fitness empire. It started with six award-winning F45 studios that really put that workout style on the map in Melbourne. After he sold them, he continued on the fitness path with Journey Retreats, a wonderful health and wellness retreat business that allows him to collaborate with some of the biggest names in the industry to create week-long meaningful escapes. He's also launched Strong, the first rowformer studio in Australia. He credits his success to the marketing and community-building skills that he developed in his formative energy career.

The three-year itch

Even if you are more certain of your way to yay and have already made a big leap towards it, yay is not so much a destination as it is an ever-unfolding journey. If I had reached my ultimate destination by starting Matcha Maiden, I would have been committing to stay statically in that role from that point onwards, without ever evolving again.

Instead, this was another step taken on the staircase without knowing of the many steps that were still to come – in directions I wouldn't have dreamed of until much later (one of those being the drastic move of opening Matcha Mylkbar). Even though the first few years of being on the matcha mission with both businesses felt fiercely passionate and full of direction, around the three- to four-year mark I found myself feeling a little lost and unsure of my direction once again.

For a little while, I fell back into the speed trap of just ticking off seemingly productive goals to appease that feeling. Nic and I went down a year-long path of business growth for the sake of growth. We prepared to open more venues and release more products without really assessing if that was the right direction for us. In fact, we have since scaled back on most of what we spent that year doing. We realised that we should have slowed down and reflected more deeply on *why* we were feeling unsure of our direction and the best way to address what came up. I have since been told this is a very common experience around the three- to four-year mark of a start-up.

Around that three-year mark, the crazy, head-down-bums-up phase of growth starts to stabilise. You officially become a 'started-up' business. This is the point when you can finally come up for air and start to think less reactively and more proactively about what might come next. As we were approaching the cusp of this new chapter, I remember feeling all the uncertainty and doubt of the beginning flood back in, and I was desperately seeking some guidance or quick answers from a more 'adultier' adult than me.

Around this time, we were very lucky to be part of the inaugural Chobani Food Incubator program which gave us six months of hands-on guidance and intimate access to the expertise of the executive team and resources of the booming yoghurt business to help us scale up. While this allowed us some fast-tracked learning and upskilling, for which I'm forever grateful, the pressure of what we 'should' do next started to creep back in.

After the program, Nic and I decided to follow in Chobani's footsteps by aggressively scaling and expanding. We spent the next year or so focusing purely on growth and volume with a view to ultimately blowing things up massively and having our products stocked in the major retailers. But, ultimately, bigger was not better for us, and the nagging inkling that this wasn't our next stepping stone continued to strengthen. It turned out that what I'd been feeling was a sense of distance between me and our ultimate customer, and that was worsening as our company was getting bigger.

The more both businesses grew, but particularly Matcha Maiden, the less involved I was in the day-to-day operations and direct interactions with people. I started to play more of an overseeing and coordinating role to make sure all the pieces were fitting together. I'd handed over direct customer service, community building and digital marketing to Ang, and given Mum the responsibility of managing all of our wholesale portfolio and supplier relationships. At the time, delegating more to make more space for working *on* the business and not always *in* it had felt like a relief. But I hadn't realised that the shift was taking me further away from the parts of the business that I enjoy most.

The oversight function I moved into is still hugely challenging, stimulating and necessary for the business to grow, and I had come nowhere near to mastering it, but it isn't the area of our work that indulges or harnesses my passion for people or love of building relationships. However, it didn't make sense for me to do anything else at that stage of our growth. A mentor once told me that you should focus on the tasks that *only* you can do and delegate the rest. It was by reflecting on ways that I could introduce more of that close interaction back into the mix in other ways (back to the journalling and mind-mapping) that the idea to start a podcast was born. And so, before I knew it, I was approaching the next step on the staircase that I hadn't seen coming. This reminded me that the uncomfortable sense of losing direction is perhaps the best alert you can get to start evaluating how you might pivot next.

For me, I think there can be a lot of guilt wrapped up in moving on from something that is already pretty wonderful and working relatively well. I'm always conscious of being grateful and actively appreciating how lucky we are to live in a world with endless choices and opportunities, which isn't a bad thing at all if it stops there. I think along with self-doubt, though, a bit of gratitude-induced guilt held me back from leaving the law firm sooner. More recently, guilt prevented me from doing any kind of work outside of the matcha mission with Matcha Maiden and Matcha Mylkbar. But, as we will come to in the next chapter, just as you grow and evolve so should the things you invest yourself in. Your first big step towards your yay will always feel a bit like your baby. But you don't have to feel bad for approaching a new chapter when you've developed and transformed to the extent that you've outgrown where you are. Being aware that this might happen and staying open-minded to the next possible steps is what makes room for new opportunities to fall in your lap.

The uncomfortable sense of losing direction is perhaps the best alert you can get to start evaluating how you might pivot next.

You can see from my story alone, the pivotal discussion points of which only really cover a five-year period so far, that the staircase cannot be bypassed to simply end up at the top from the beginning. I would never have been able to jump straight into recording *Seize the Yay* when I finished university, nor would anyone have listened to me having had no life experience to base anything on at that point. I now feel more aligned and directed than ever thanks to the balance of different things I'm able to work on. And I'm still learning about my purpose and passion in the process. Your staircase is ever unfolding. It's malleable and will bend to your will if you let go of needing to see all of it at once.

I'm completely open-minded and appreciative of the fact that what I need and what needs me is likely to change many times in the coming years and throughout my life. That's the beauty of the dynamic life we are so lucky to live today. I've gone from having a five-year plan to barely having a five-minute plan. As Rachel Kelly, one of our mentors, so perfectly expressed, 'Every next level of your life demands a different you.' It's just about staying patient and open-minded while you figure out what those levels and versions of you are.

CHAPTER 8

Welcome to the discomfort zone

With all this talk of staircases and stepping stones, the question has probably arisen in your mind as to how you incite or determine a change in direction or choose the next best step in your current direction. This brings me back to an ongoing theme of seizing your yay: the most important thing is that you pay close attention to yourself and how certain things make you *feel* – which may be vastly different at different stages of your life.

It sounds painfully simple, yet so many of us rarely stop to evaluate ourselves and pay attention to the signs that provide so many of the answers we need. With Matcha Maiden, for example, there were signs for months before I thought of starting a podcast that I was missing the human connection element of our work. I was that girl who always wanted a face-to-face meeting about something that could have been an email for a long while. I found myself reaching out to loyal customers or suppliers through my personal channels to touch base and connect. I'm still guilty of forgetting to check in with myself much of the time and often look back on certain periods of change realising the writing had been on the wall for far longer than I realised.

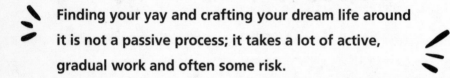

Finding your yay and crafting your dream life around it is not a passive process; it takes a lot of active, gradual work and often some risk.

I used to think finding my passion was something that would strike me one day, and I was waiting like an eager beaver for that moment to arrive. While it's not unheard of for people to have a middle-of-the-night epiphany or similar, most of us need to work a little harder to uncover where we should go next. Finding your yay and crafting your dream life around it is not a passive process; it takes a lot of active, gradual work and often some risk. Much like mining gemstones, there's a lot of crap to wade through and some blood, sweat and tears to be shed, but if you make a concerted effort, you can ultimately dig through and find what you're looking for.

Comfort in discomfort

A quote I always find helpful here is from Thomas Jefferson, 'If you want something you've never had, you must be willing to do something you've never done.' It probably won't surprise you that this quote is also a favourite of Samantha Gash, the friend who first introduced me to the joys of the discomfort zone. Again, like many things that we need regular and gentle reminding of, it seems obvious in the abstract (but much harder to apply in practice) that nothing changes if nothing changes. You can't find out what things you like or don't like until you've tried those things and you won't know your real limits until you attempt to push yourself to them. This is why they say that comfort zones are great but nothing exciting ever really happens there – they generally involve the constant repetition of routines and behaviours that aren't really going to grow you even if they maintain you. And so, if you're not particularly enamoured with your current direction and feel you're not quite seizing your yay, it's probably time to starting shaking shit up.

Before we go any further, I've got another disclaimer: sometimes the comfort zone is *exactly* where you need to be and is where you should allow yourself to hang for a bit. There are circumstances or things that happen in life that are challenging and consuming enough to make working on your direction or personal development a much lower priority. Family illnesses, unexpected trauma or anything similar can cause serious disruption and distress and require your full emotional and physical attention. If you're going through or recovering from something like this, you absolutely deserve time to just recoup and rejuvenate in the most comfortable way you can. In my case, my stint in Hong Kong was a time in my life where I allowed myself to put the brakes on a little and focus on living the experience I was having. I mentally allocated it as time to just enjoy each day without trying to be the *best* at it or work out what came next, which is how I had approached my career until that point.

Admittedly, I was still in a great position at a fantastic international law firm, so I wasn't exactly bludging over there. But, I did let go of my traditional need to achieve and excel to instead coast comfortably because I had been so unwell with my parasite before I got there. I was still 15 kilograms underweight from the effects of the parasite when I arrived in Hong Kong, and had a lot of healing to do. It wasn't the right time to delve into butcher's paper mind maps of my future plans – but a year-and-a-half later, once I was strong and had recovered, the idea for Matcha Maiden got scribbled out on a serviette.

Assuming you *are* in a good place for seizing your yay, the best thing you can do is actively explore your strengths and weaknesses, likes and dislikes, delights and fears. I was once so disconnected with these kinds of internal discussions that it's no wonder I wasn't sure where I was headed – I'd only ever seriously considered one route up the corporate legal ladder. All other options were barely more than hypothetical. I remember chatting about career possibilities outside of law with one of my colleagues. They asked me a simple question about what it was that I liked or enjoyed and it still blows my mind to remember that I couldn't answer their question. I had no idea what I loved doing because I made no time or brain space for any activities outside of work, sleep and catching up with friends.

It took me a very lengthy process of reverse engineering to work out the basic things that made me feel good and distinguish those from the things that didn't interest me at all. Since I didn't intrinsically know what they were, I had to observe myself like a third party: I'd identify times when I was happy or excited and then work backwards to figure out what it was about those moments that made me enjoy them. It makes me laugh so much now but I literally bought a journal and wrote down what I was doing every time I noticed I felt invigorated or positive or when I felt the opposite. After a few months of gathering data (yes, on myself. I did say it could take some great lengths to get to know yourself), I then went back through those journals entries to work out who I was and what I liked most by the process of deduction.

If this sounds like you – unable to clearly identify what things you enjoy the most and what you don't – it might take quite a lot of dedicated work and attention to discover what suits you best. As weird as it sounds, at one point I felt like a total stranger to myself and was unable to answer basic questions about what I liked, wanted or was interested in. A consistent exploration of yourself is always going to be useful and help reveal more parts of the puzzle. Kristina Karlsson encourages working for free or volunteering (if you are in the position to be able to) to get a true hands-on insight into what might or might not be your thing.

Through this process, I've gone from being a great lover of my comfort zone to a discomfort junkie. I'm always seeking out new things to test myself against because I now appreciate so much that I don't know what I don't know. In recent years, under Nic and Ang's spontaneous influence, I'm always keen to give new things a red-hot crack knowing that, in some cases, I'll find out I'm completely useless at something (pottery) or that I dislike it immensely (bouldering). In other cases, however, I'll end up stumbling on a new area of enjoyment or growth. It helps enormously if you have friends around you who are equally as adventurous and will go on self-discovery, fact-finding missions with you.

The people around you can also be helpful in this exercise by providing an objective, outsider's insight into what they might think you enjoy the most or seem lit up by. What you can't think through or observe yourself, your friends, family or even colleagues might be able to shed more practical light on. Once we started Matcha Maiden, it was amazing how many family members and friends around us have expressed that they always felt I would start to miss indulging my creative side and how they think our life in business is well-suited to me. My first reaction was why on earth nobody had bothered to mention this when I was first starting to search for more yay outside of the law. I realised, later, however that I had never bothered to ask those around me to help me fill in the picture of who I was and what I should do. I didn't know anyone else had noticed I had lost a bit of sparkle, so it always pays to ask those around you while you search for your yay.

One of my favourite ways to dip my toe into new waters is to do it in the literal sense and go overseas. If you have the chance and your circumstances allow for it, travelling broadly and beyond your cultural familiarity will teach you more about yourself and the world than any other experience can. When I was at uni, there was a Monash

Abroad program available to us which provided financial grants and the possibility of gaining credits towards your degree with partner universities overseas. The university heavily prioritised overseas experiences to build worldliness and development in us, and I worked four jobs during my degree to support five different exchanges. I spent time in Japan, China and three separate exchanges to France, including almost a year studying at Sciences Politiques in Paris, completing parts of my law degree in French. As well as invaluable advances in my language abilities, I can attribute my biggest personal breakthroughs to those periods away from home.

You already know how impactful my stint in Hong Kong was on our journey to yay and the discovery of matcha that led to a total change in direction. Our travels into completely different cultures in Asia, India and Africa especially have exposed Nic and I to thoughts and perspectives we never could have had in the comfort and familiarity of our lives back home. The trips I did alone were the most reflective and transformative, for the lows more so than the highs, but also for the separation from your comfortable routines and habits that you never otherwise take the chance to really evaluate or tweak. I feel very lucky that we are so compatible in our prioritising of travel in the budget over physical purchases. I'd give up all my clothes for a travel experience purely because of the unrivalled chance it gives you to get to know yourself anew.

Having said that, the transformative moments might not always come from the brand-new or drastic things you try, but from existing things you didn't realise you enjoyed so much until you sat down to give it some thought. In fact, one of the things that inspired my using the word 'yay' is how it calls out to our inner child. In so many of our podcast episodes and broader discussions, hindsight reveals how we often come back to the things we gravitated towards as unencumbered, open-minded children. In many situations, that involves a big diversion down a 'should'-driven path that leads further and further away from the things we loved in our purest state before something makes you realise it's not actually suited to you and you go back to what you started with before obligation, responsibility and adulthood intervened.

 Transformative moments might not come from the brand-new or drastic things you try, but from existing things you didn't realise you enjoyed so much.

My childhood, for example, was filled with interesting and different people, interactions and a great mix of hardcore academic interests with equally strong tendencies towards the artistic and creative. Everything I'm doing now makes complete sense against that background and reflects the interests from my childhood, whereas my law career matched only one isolated part of my personality. Now that I think about it, I really had all the information I needed from my childhood about what lights me up and what elements I should look to incorporate into my world for a fulfilling, exciting life. Looking back to your earlier years (or even asking loved ones around you about that time) can sometimes be instructive when working out your pathyay.

Another thing that sparks new ideas and next steps for many people is simply observing their surroundings, not only to get an idea of what they're passionate about, but also to show them what they *could* be passionate about applying themselves to. So many business ideas, including Matcha Maiden, are sparked when a small, personal, regular frustration arises and the person seeks to address that gap in the market for themselves. Triangl Swimwear, for example, was founded out of a simple frustration at the lack of appropriately affordable and appealing swimwear for a first date on the beach. While this frustration-easing approach may not necessarily show you what you're passionate about or invigorated by *directly*, it can change your focus and activity in a way that later reveals things about yourself you didn't otherwise know.

For me, the gap led to Matcha Maiden in that it highlighted *by contrast* what I enjoyed. It showed how law *wasn't* bringing out the best version of me, whereas our surprise business idea activated areas of my brain and personality I hadn't seen in years. It suddenly became part of my job to draw things, design labels and write creatively with a freedom not permitted when writing contracts. I was constantly innovating to create products that made people feel good (although I might not have known I'd enjoy that without first seeking to close a gap in the market).

I certainly wasn't a legal expert by then, not by any means, but the learning curve in law had slowed, and the opportunity for new ideas and creativity was scarce. Business, however, opened me up to a dynamic, fast-paced, constantly evolving environment. Every day required me to pivot or adapt to new conditions. I didn't know until I was thrown into it that my brain thrived on this type of work. Each stage of that first business, and the subsequent businesses, has opened up new dimensions and shown me different things that make me yay.

Another great example of stumbling across a new form of yay through closing a gap in the market is the podcast *Shameless*, started by two wonderful Melbourne journalists

Zara McDonald and Michelle Andrews. Dubbed the 'podcast for smart women who love dumb stuff', it's a refreshingly honest, heavily researched and politically savvy podcast covering the celebrity news cycle in a meaningful way – a type of commentary not widely available at the time it launched. The idea came about when the two were working as writers at media company Mamamia. They were overheard having a sophisticated and deep conversation about *The Bachelor* and then given a chance to cut their podcast teeth on an internal podcast comprising twice-weekly 10-minute slots and named, *Bach Chat*. In the process, they realised they'd stumbled upon something special, so they prepared several ideas to pitch to their superiors at Mamamia. Their initial pitch for *Shameless* was rejected, but they started the podcast independently and it grew so quickly that both of them were later able to make the transition to working on *Shameless* full time.

Their podcast has now been downloaded millions of times and received all kinds of recognition, including becoming the nation's most popular podcast at the Australian Podcast Awards. I love being in the podcast space with these two clever cookies, we've been on each other's shows several times and I'm chuffed that they often refer to *Seize the Yay* as a 'sister pod'. Through the extraordinary growth, Michelle and Zara have been able to uncover the topics and work they are truly passionate about and develop an unrestricted, direct way to share those with their millions of twice-weekly listeners rather than simply through their writing. The work they do in their community and beyond has expanded to things like becoming ambassadors for various causes close to their heart. While closing a gap in the market that has been extraordinary well received, they also uncovered a means to make their passions their profession at the same time. This is just one of many stories that unfold this way.

The next mountain

Another quote I turn to often – which happens to come from the title of Lola Yayo's book on hiking – is, 'If you think you've peaked find a new mountain.' What took me a few years to learn is that your comfort zone is ever-evolving, just like everything in life. So even if you do take a step outside it, eventually your comfort zone will catch up to you and you'll have to step outside it again to find new parts of yourself. That once new, scary thing will eventually feel comfortable and familiar as you grow and develop into that next chapter of your life – and, as we discussed, you don't have to feel guilty about this process of stretching and growing.

Once I stepped out of law and into Matcha Maiden, I became a little overly self-congratulatory – kind of ticking off a big, scary jump as if it was the last one I'd ever need to make. I (naively) thought that doing this had unearthed every previously undiscovered corner of my passions and interests. While I clearly hadn't 'won' business or learned every single thing I'd ever need to learn through becoming an entrepreneur, I was slowly realising that the evolution of my role over time allowed less and less personal interaction with customers, suppliers and other stakeholders in our community, which is what truly lights me up. Consequently, the business as a whole was losing its sparkle for me, because the part I loved the most was no longer part of my job.

And so, a few years later, it came time to find a new mountain in order to address what I now realised was a big part of what made my work fulfilling to me: personal connection. I went back to the drawing board and came up with the idea for the *Seize the Yay* podcast. We must continually take these steps out of our comfort zone throughout our lives to discover more and more about ourselves and recognise what our next best steps are. Some of you might stumble upon a whole career or other major life change in the process of doing this. Others may end up more like me: waiting with an open mind so I'm ready when the next step pops up quite unexpectedly. The next step might literally fall into your lap, but if you haven't been doing the work to explore what best suits you, you may not be able to identify and take advantage of it.

You can't start the next chapter if you keep re-reading the last

A big thing I have noticed over the past few years of change is how much we are conditioned by our past selves when we start to explore who else we might become. Though reflecting on what made you joyful as a child can be a great thing to do, it can also leave you stuck in a certain way of seeing yourself that makes it very hard to allow yourself to be something different. My mum, for example, grew up in a time where women chose teaching or nursing – entrepreneurship wasn't a word most people were familiar with. She spent most of her life with those boundaries restricting her potential career paths or even her consideration of what was possible, and yet, when Matcha Maiden started to truly blossom, she became our full-time chief operating officer. She was endlessly capable of either fulfilling the role as it was or upskilling to learn what she needed to, but the biggest challenge wasn't teaching her these skills, it was helping her see herself as someone capable of working in a tech-focused digital-heavy start-up without an office space, corporate structure or business plan. I often had to remind her about wise words spoken by . . . a wise unknown author: you can't start reading the next chapter if you keep re-reading the last.

Agapi Stassinopoulos talks about these kinds of limiting self-beliefs in *Wake Up to the Joy of You*, using her dating life as an example. She believed that men would disappoint her because of a belief she had that was rooted in her mother's disappointment in Agapi's father. Because of this belief, Agapi wound up attracting men who were emotionally unavailable and as a result she ended up feeling disappointed and making her belief true! This self-fulfilling prophecy can apply to all kinds of self-limiting, backwards-facing opinions or attitudes about ourselves. If we stay rooted in our past identities or preconceptions about what we're able or unable to do, we'll never be open to pushing ourselves to new and different limits. Our earlier exploration into self-doubt and the vital importance of a positive mindset applies here in the same way to help clear your pathyay from the mental obstacles of self-underestimation. As Shelley Laslett reminded me during our chat about mindset, we must be careful about the stories we tell ourselves and remember we can (and should) re-write them to suit our goals.

You don't, of course, need to start a *whole* new chapter or let go of your former self every time you stumble across something that isn't bringing you yay. The parts of your life that might be working perfectly well can be safeguarded from any drastic changes. My lovely friend Cath Daish (née Hillis) started off in corporate law at a similar top-tier international firm to the one I worked at. Like me, she spent several years working incredibly long hours before realising corporate law was not the right pathway for her. She didn't necessarily dislike law altogether so she didn't need close the legal chapter entirely (although she could still have felt limited by her conception of herself as a corporate lawyer rather than any other kind). She did, however, move successfully out of corporate law and into the completely different realm of family law, where she now works on cases she is passionate about and, consequently, she's absolutely thriving.

 We must be careful about the stories we tell ourselves and remember we can (and should) re-write them to suit our goals.

Another amazing woman who's made a similar sideways move and is seizing her yay *within* law is Amy Serpless (née Barber). Amy started her career in corporate law at the same firm as Samantha Gash who introduced me to her (and we both became Samantha's bridesmaids along with Prue Smith from the same firm). All three of their careers have provided a lot of guidance for me. Amy left the corporate world just before Samantha and headed into the wonderful world of diplomacy and international law. She ended up working in what would have been a dream job for me had I stayed in law: working with the United Nations in countries such as Tanzania, Cambodia and Liberia. When those positions finished up, she returned to Australia and took up a position as a public prosecutor.

Amy is also now a part-time legal officer in the Army Reserves. In her spare time, she teaches yoga at a local women's prison in Perth. Meanwhile, Prue jumped from corporate to a position with the United Nations (you can see why these women have been so inspiring to me). You don't always have to make a complete jump outside your existing career to change something *inside* it for the better.

Navigating the forks in the road

While a lot of the self-exploration we've discussed is quite a gradual process, it is not uncommon for many of us to encounter our next step in the form of a huge fork in the road. When this happens, there is usually some risk involved. Sometimes, the opportunity to create the life of your dreams presents as an all-or-nothing decision.

The glaring crossroads situation that I get asked about the most is when I had to choose whether to remain a lawyer or to go full time with Matcha Maiden and leave my job completely. How did I build up the courage to leave the respectable, sensible job I had studied nearly a decade to prepare for? Was it the scariest thing I've ever done and how did I overcome that fear? How did I know Matcha Maiden would be successful enough to sustain my livelihood?

So much of our decision-making in life is dominated by 'should': what does society/my family/the world think I *should* be doing at this point? Rarely do we sit and reflect on what we *want* to do and what that looks like day-to-day. Even though nobody was directly telling me what I should do, I was so bogged down in trying to figure out the sensible thing to do, or what sounded best on a macro level. At one point, I even considered applying for further study at Oxford or Cambridge because a Master of Law would look great on my CV. Thankfully, I've started to look at things in a much more microscopic, day-to-day way: *Do I actually want to go live in England for a few years away from my family and loved ones to work my absolute butt off studying about a subject matter I'm not sure I'm delighted by just because it sounds good?'*

'Should' thinking often leads us towards doing things that are comfortable, familiar and predictable and, don't get me wrong, those things are still important factors to consider when creating a beautiful life. But the gap between what things *sound* like and what they *feel* like to experience is what I believe ends up causing so much unhappiness and dissatisfaction for people when they live out their decisions. In the context of Matcha Maiden, 'should' is what led us to believe that unqualified growth and expansion was necessarily positive. The bigger your financial turnover, distribution and volume, the fancier and more successful your business sounds, which must be a good thing, right?

But once I flipped my thinking towards the micro, day-to-day level of what this decision actually meant for us, I realised that a major scale-up would change my job description and our whole structure completely in ways that didn't necessarily suit our personal definitions of yay. For me, scaling up would mean spending most of my days in a high-vis vest pacing around a factory that would send us into enormous debt to set up and run. And that debt would mean much less scope and ability to adapt and innovate. If you're looking purely at numbers (which, as you can probably guess, I wasn't), scaling up also meant that we'd have overall lower profit margins for quite some years, even if our actual revenue from sales was greater. Even without that numerical logic, though, we realised that what looks good from the outside and what feels good on the daily aren't always the same.

Breaking a personal deadlock

In many cases, running through this type of macro/micro analysis can help provide guidance on whatever situation you are pulled towards. When I'm faced with big decisions, I usually turn to a broader pros-and-cons analysis, slotting the macro and micro considerations into their appropriate columns. The decision-making matrix is a complicated, layered exercise, and again, yours might look very different to mine. The metaphorical butcher's paper gets a real thrashing on your way to yay, but it's all in the name of building your best life with all the information you can gather.

Even the smaller, less-significant decisions in our life are generally made with reference to this simple pros and cons or 'cost–benefit analysis' balancing act. The trouble is that some crossroads-type situations end up with relatively balanced columns or without enough concrete information for the columns to be accurate. There are exciting, probably life-changing, benefits to taking a risk but there are also stability, certainty and security benefits to maintaining the status quo. So, how do you break a decision-making deadlock?

I've found one question to be the most helpful in situations like this, and particularly when I decided whether to leave law: what is the once-in-a-lifetime opportunity? If the merits of each option are hard to balance but you can only choose one right now, which one is the opportunity you will never be able to come back to? For me, I had worked hard to build what I hoped was a strong professional reputation so, ultimately, I was likely to be able to come back to a job in law if things didn't work out in business. Lawyers are as sure a thing as death and taxes in this life, and the industry wasn't going anywhere. Additionally, I had realised from looking at my superiors in the firm that I didn't, in fact, aspire to be in their positions. Probably a fairly good indication that it was time to change paths.

By contrast, giving Matcha Maiden a 'red-hot crack' was a very temporal opportunity – it was unlikely to present itself the same way again. Of course, you can start a company any time, but the chance to build a company and be one of the first to market at a time when demand is increasing exponentially in a global landscape is extremely rare.

So, my decision-making matrix became more of a regret-management matrix. I have since realised that this is why I have very few (if any) major regrets in life. Working through this type of decision-making exercise covers all my bases, so I know I'm never (or hopefully, very rarely) making decisions out of habit, default or fear. If things don't work out, I know I've considered my options and consciously chosen to take that risk. Seen in this light, leaving law was very low risk in the scheme of things as it was unlikely to be something I would later regret.

If things hadn't worked out with Matcha Maiden, I could have very likely reversed the effects of my decision. I could have coped with being several months behind my peers on the career ladder. But if the business worked out, then it was worth the risk all along. However, if I didn't take a chance on Matcha Maiden, I would have always wondered how great it could have been, and I never would have known it would surpass our wildest hopes and dreams. On balance, the decision to leave my law career ended up being easier to decide than I thought it would be. Of course, it was *scary*, but this exercise made it clear that this was the right decision for me at that time.

Mind you, this is me reflecting with half a decade's worth of hindsight; I'm not sure Nic will remember me being quite so resolved. A few years later, after some of the dust had settled, I realised this was me choosing to seize my yay. As you now know, I was struck by that terminology in 2017 when I immediately registered it. That said, I've probably been in the process of developing the concept since much earlier, when I started putting it into practice.

The 'associated' risk

There was one small thing that did throw a bit of a spanner in the works, and that was that I wasn't just walking away from the law firm – I was also walking away from a bigger, rarer opportunity that I'd almost forgotten about. I mentioned that the trajectory of a legal career often starts way back at university, and back then I had applied for what's called a judge's associateship.

Each judge in the various courts has one or more associates, usually for a year at a time, to assist them with anything from researching decisions to picking up their dry cleaning, depending on the judge. It doesn't sound it, but it's a highly sought-after position in law that you take up a few years into your career – you take a year off then go back to your original job. It's more of a developmental experience that sets you up especially well if you want to work in the courts yourself.

In my student days, my 'just ask, the worst they can say is no' approach was in its early development, but it was present enough that I applied straight to the High Court – the highest court in the Australian judicial system. These positions are even more coveted because there are so few High Court judges (only seven at any one time). I applied to several judges and went through some very lengthy application processes to ultimately be turned down by all of them. I was disappointed, but quickly moved on and turned my focus to writing my final year honours thesis and living my life.

My thesis happened to aggressively dissect one of the High Court judgments of Chief Justice Susan Kiefel

(Justice Kiefel at the time). I still don't know whether Her Honour read my thesis, or if what followed was a coincidence, but, a little while after my thesis was published in an academic journal, I was offered a position with her commencing in early 2016 after someone pulled out. I accepted, then didn't think of it again until years later when deciding whether or not to jump full time into Matcha Maiden. By then, my start date had crept up and I was due to move up to Brisbane (Her Honour's home jurisdiction) to begin just six months later.

If I was walking away from law, then I would also have to turn down this coveted clerkship. And while my corporate job wasn't a once-in-a-lifetime opportunity, being an associate to the Chief Justice of the highest court in the country *definitely* was. You can imagine how complicated this decision was with this layer added to it, and I'm forever grateful to Nic, Mum and the many friends I earbashed while I worked though it all. In the end, you know which decision I made. I won't pretend it didn't feel world-ending at the time, but I haven't regretted it for a moment.

I worked through my macro/micro analysis again and thought long and hard about what I *really* wanted to spend the next 18 months of my life doing. On a macro level, the prestige and experience of being intimately involved with the High Court was hard to resist. On a micro level, though, it meant moving away from family and friends for a year and spending most of my days buried in case law with only one colleague for company. By this time, we'd been running Matcha Maiden for six months, and I'd been exposed to the different ways that business activated my creative passions in a way that law didn't. The move interstate would necessitate the complete closure of Matcha Maiden, and it was going too well to walk away from. So, I chose not to, thank goodness.

I guess what I'm realising even as I write these words is that seizing your yay is equal parts dedicated effort on the one hand and surrender on the other. I feel so sure that building the Seize the Yay brand, community, podcast and world is what I am meant to be doing right now, but it has taken five years of constant self-inquiry – from the first revelation that led to Matcha Maiden, which itself took me 25 years to reach. I also feel sure that the new brand and my role within it will change constantly, but I have to surrender to the process and remain open-minded in order to allow the unexpected, delightful and exciting to come into the picture. Finding my own yay has been, and will continue to be, an evolving, unfolding process. But I don't need to see the whole staircase to keep taking steps. I trust that each step is as important as the last in making me who I am destined to become.

CHAPTER 9

Failing forwards

What would a book about seizing your yay be if it didn't acknowledge the uncomfortable but unavoidable topic of failure? And what type of successful person would you be if you hadn't experienced at least one, if not many, serious setbacks to get there? Something I have come to understand is that while some situations are undoubtedly a 'failure' in the sense that they cause you to lose money or don't achieve any of their objectives, overall you can reframe most failures in a way that allows you to make peace with the discomfort they cause and focus instead on the lessons you learned. Everything can be seen through a new yay-frame; you just have to learn to see these so-called 'failures' in a way that works to your advantage rather than your disadvantage.

Having a yay-type attitude isn't necessarily something you're born with, but it is something you can cultivate.

Taking a step backwards can still be a step in the right direction in the sense that it teaches you about something that *doesn't* work and provides you with an opportunity to do it better next time around. There are no foundations quite as strong as rock bottom; as I like to remind myself, the very best views often come after the hardest climb. It's extremely handy for this chapter that almost every guest we've had on *Seize the Yay* so far has experienced an apparent failure-turned-transformative learning – I like to call this 'failing forwards'.

At the time of writing, for example, Lisa Messenger has recently closed her once-wildly-successful print edition of *Collective Hub* magazine, which might initially have felt like a massive fail. The subsequent pivot from print to greener pastures (and her signature openness about it) is such that Lisa has already released a fabulous book documenting her learnings in detail: *Risk & Resilience*. Like all her books, it's an insightful, honest and practical read. As the very first sentence so beautifully describes, 'When you're deep in the middle of a total and utter, mind-scrambling cluster-f*ck is when the best ideas materialise.' Under what she describes as 'the pressure of scaling too quickly, hiring too rapidly, over-promising without adequate resources, not employing right-hand people early enough and letting our egos take over' (i.e. the 'bigger is better' mentality we too fell into with Matcha Maiden that we spoke about in chapter 7), Collective Hub nearly sank. At one point, it was losing A$150,000 a month and Lisa ended up sinking more than A$1 million of her personal funds into keeping the business afloat.

The very best views often come after the hardest climb.

Rather than seeing this as a sign to shut up shop and throw in the towel, Lisa chose to focus on the silver linings, which she then shared for the benefit of others. She even included honest figures and financials to show how she could bring the business back and make it even better and more efficient than before. Lisa is one of my favourite writers, especially on the topics of failure and resilience, and she often reminds me that the comeback is always stronger than the setback. One of the practical strategies Lisa details in *Risk & Resilience* is to start by addressing your issues head-on so you know exactly what you're dealing with and then act quickly and scale down fast in order to salvage what you still can. Avoiding your issues is much easier in the short term but addressing the reality upfront as early as you are able to can liberate you from fear of the unknown and allow you to do something about it.

The next strategy Lisa suggests is to spend some time getting clear again on your core vision and coming back to what matters most. Finally, once you get clear on that, start to reframe the ending. In her case, this involved closing the print magazine but founding a new iteration of *Collective Hub* – just delivered differently. The new iteration pursues the same core values, but via new and different delivery methods, which of course includes her brand-new podcast as well as other digital resources and physical merchandise. Lisa's tried-and-tested technique is to 'fail fast', forget the mistake but remember the lesson and get back to where you want to be as quickly as you can. Lisa and I often chat about how everything in life unfolds in iterations or chapters over time, so a failure of one iteration or version of your idea or business is just the key to the improvement of the next version of it.

Lisa is an inspiring reminder to me not to waste time and energy beating myself up about something that hasn't worked so well, but instead focus on shifting quickly and effectively towards bettering the next thing. There are so many other examples out there of successful people who have had failures that either result in the improvement of what they do or, like Lisa, that involves cutting off *parts* of what they do and pivoting into something better (thereby failing forwards). In other cases, however, success has come from resisting failure completely and refusing to see it as fatal. One of my favourite examples of this resilience is J.K. Rowling, creator of the ubiquitous Harry Potter.

To know me is to know that I am a huge Harry Potter fan (and a very proud Gryffindor). Although I cannot fathom a single reason why, the Harry Potter series was initially rejected by 12 different publishers before the chairman of Bloomsbury gave his eight-year-old daughter the first chapter to read. Bloomsbury agreed to publish the book, but advised J.K. that she was unlikely to make money in children's books. Instead, she went from being a jobless, single mother living on unemployment benefits to the first female billionaire author in the world. I get shivers thinking about what might have happened if she had taken the 10th or 11th publisher's rejection as fatal and abandoned the idea for Harry Potter without ever knowing what it could become – I know my childhood would have been very different.

To date, that book series has been translated into 73 languages, sold millions of copies and accrued over US$20 billion through movie deals and the like. Even so, J.K. has explained that, in her past, she was the biggest failure that she knew. In her Harvard commencement address, J.K. told the graduates that the only way they'd avoid failure in life is if they lived so carefully that they couldn't fail – in which case, they may as well not have lived at all.

In Matcha Maiden's case, there have been so many situations that would count as failures, but we've learned to use those to help propel us forward. We've experienced many rejections after pitches or meetings; sure, these haven't been quite on the scale of J.K. Rowling's as they didn't have the potential to end Matcha Maiden altogether, but they definitely left us feeling defeated and uncertain about our ability to succeed. But more commonly, our failures have been less external rejections and more internal screw-ups on our part.

Quite a few of our failures have involved us either under- or over-preparing for a situation then being left with too little or too much of something – usually in a way that had big financial ramifications. One example of this that I still get reminded of regularly is the great cardboard box incident of 2018. The boxes are still sitting in our office smirking at me every day (or they would be if boxes could smirk). They were ordered during that period I talked about where Nic and I got sidetracked by the 'bigger is better' mentality. We became aggressively focused on economies of scale and preparing for drastic growth, and though we have sent out single bags of matcha in flat, postal satchels since we started Matcha Maiden, we decided (without doing any real research) that boxes would be more professional. They'd also allow us to create packs of one, two and three bags to help increase the cart value per customer. We hastily sourced some cardboard boxes that were an absolute bargain . . . if you ordered 10,000 at a time.

That's the point of economies of scale: as you order bigger quantities, you can access heavily discounted pricing, so as you grow things become more cost-effective. But for that equation to actually work, you not only have to be sure you're going to use 10,000 boxes, you also need to know that posting them out isn't going to cost a fortune. Well, in our haste, we didn't calculate how these boxes would impact our postage price. And, delightfully, the boxes cost almost 500 per cent more to post than our flat satchels. Since Matcha Maiden offers free shipping, we would be wearing this increase in price. Needless to say, we ended up using less than 5 per cent of those boxes; rather than being extremely cost effective at less than 50 cents each, those 500 boxes ended up costing us about A$10 each!

Our failures have been less external rejections and more internal screw-ups on our part. Quite a few of these involved us either under- or over-preparing for a situation.

In the grand scheme of things, this box incident might not sound extreme, but when you're a growing a start-up, dropping thousands of dollars on something you don't use *could* sink you financially. Cash flow is often so tight in the growth phase of a business that even small mistakes can affect your finances in a way that have a knock-on effect on your abilities to pay bills, pay staff, purchase stock or any other number of things for months or even years. This box debacle definitely felt like a failure for us, particularly as the flow-on effects lasted for months; we had to borrow from our personal funds to buy our next batch of matcha, and we were unable to pay that loan back for months until we finally re-established a profit. However, this taught us such valuable lessons about over-extending ourselves and making decisions too hastily before we grew even further and made the same mistake on a much bigger and, potentially more damaging, purchase.

Nic and I have also gone as far as releasing new products that ended up being a huge pain to sell and resulted in a considerable loss for our business (not to mention a major excess for us to consume ourselves). Some of these misses, such as products we launched far too hastily, were avoidable, but others surprised us because not only had we had done our market research, but these specific products had even been requested by our customers. But, in the end, they just didn't work on a large scale, and sometimes our stockists were unable to sell even their first order. On reflection, we didn't invest heavily enough in supportive education campaigns to tell our customers how these new products differed to regular matcha; we treated the views of a few customers as being representative of the whole market. We now know that you can get too far into your own business bubble that you hear only the voices of your existing community and customer base. We also learned that there's a very fine balance between being constantly ahead of the curve, on one hand, and also waiting for the market to be ready for what you've developed, on the other. Finding this sweet spot is something we still grapple with today.

There are many other instances where we've failed, some more severe, some less, and many of these have understandably brought on feelings of shame, inadequacy or disappointment in us. Some have also caused conflict between Nic and I when we've been distracted by playing the blame game. But, after the dust has settled and we've had time to reflect, every one of these situations has taught us a lesson; they've helped us refine and improve our systems in a way that avoided much bigger, more serious consequences later on when we grew bigger.

Since moving into podcasting, presenting and other work that involves my personal profile, setbacks or failures have hit even harder as the product is no longer an inanimate bag of matcha, but *me*. Failure can feel personal, and on a bad day, it can lead you to question why you're even doing what you're doing. There have been many times that a mistake has overwhelmed me and made me consider throwing in the towel. But, as I've learned from Lisa and the other people around me, the best thing I can do when I face failure is get my perspective back as soon as I can, look for the silver linings and bounce back with any learnings to be gleaned so I can do better next time.

If you're in a business partnership as Nic and I are (particularly with your actual partner), it is so important to acknowledge each other's disappointment and emotion, but also to set aside time once things have calmed down to review what happened and identify what you can learn from it together. We definitely haven't always been the best at dealing with setbacks or failure (separately or together), but over time we have realised that our greatest strength isn't necessarily how we deal with the good times, but how we bounce back from the bad times. You have a choice at these moments to let a setback get the better of you or to push back harder next time. Just keep coming back to the yay-frame and remember that you control your emotions, not the other way around.

When failure gets personal

While Nic and I have developed quite strong strategies for bouncing back from business setbacks, my personal failures have been greater and tougher to recover from. People often ask if I've experienced any major moments of failure in my journey and though the learnings from our business failures have been immeasurable, they aren't the ones I think of first. My major failure has been managing my own health and wellbeing through the transition from my working environments, despite that exact problem being what led to the start of our businesses in the first place. Having been driven by a bout of self-inflicted adrenal fatigue from overwork and ignoring the importance of pacing myself to start our business, I somehow ended up in this exact same place a few years into our business.

Towards the end of 2016, without realising, I had almost managed to turn our Matcha Maiden working environment into a corporate one. Because we were so passionate about the business I was smashing myself in much the same way as I had been at the law firm, and I was ignoring the signs of burnout yet again. Without meaning to, I had somehow crept back onto the productivity hamster wheel and re-merged my sense of self-worth with output and busyness.

I fell back into an unrelenting work cycle, never giving myself a break or practising the message of health and wellbeing that our business was preaching. When I finally went to the doctor, I was told I had relapsed into adrenal fatigue again, only this time the sporadic panic attacks that had surfaced after Africa had escalated into severe anxiety. This dual diagnosis felt like such a huge personal failure because this time around I'd had all the tools to avoid it but had completely neglected to exercise them.

It took me almost a year to fully recover from this health setback, which made it difficult to put any of the failing strategies I'd learned about into practice; I wasn't able to 'fail fast' and put this behind me that quickly. At my worst, I was as unwell as I had been after our African trip – completely bedridden and lethargic, but this time with the added layer of severe anxiety. Faced with not only physical symptoms but also emotional ones, I felt completely out of my depth. My body might have failed me before, but my brain had never refused to cooperate.

It took drastic attention to restoring my physical and mental wellbeing for me to make even small steps of improvement, and unfortunately this meant I had a lot of time to let the feelings of failure engulf me. Years later, I was eventually able to see that while that trip taught me about my physical limits, this major setback taught me that I also had emotional and mental limits to work around. I had never actively looked after my brain separately to my body, and was therefore pushing it to all kinds of limits without realising. The end result was that I was forced to go back to zero to build things back up.

As well as returning to very clean nutrition, getting as much sleep and rest as possible and adopting all the same physical measures I had when I recovered after Africa, I also had to quickly become acquainted with what it takes to look after your mind. I started meditating every day and limited emotional and mental stimulation in order to give my brain a break and a chance to recover. Even if I tried, I could hardly work or use devices at all without becoming overwhelmed with anxiety. This gave me a pretty clear warning that I had overloaded myself and that my body was now forcing me away from the things I'd been overdoing. It wasn't one particular thing, like social media or work emails, that triggered me, it was just generally the prospect of thinking or interacting that overwhelmed me. I now realise that my mind has a general overstimulation limit and, given that I didn't know that existed, I had been living over that line my whole life — in the digital world *and* the real world.

And when I say I became 'overwhelmed with anxiety', I don't just mean I felt stressed or as though it was all a bit much; I mean I was literally overcome physiologically and unable to do anything further. It's so hard to explain that feeling if you haven't experienced it, but I often use this analogy to help: it's as though the police call you and tell you that something has happened to a loved one, but they have no information or details to give you so you have to wait for another call. Imagine how you would feel waiting for that next call – it's not just emotional concern or worry, but completely physical-churning with all your insides knotted up and an impending sense of doom that something is about to happen, you just don't know what. This was the feeling I was living with at that time, and it crippled my ability to function properly. It would get worse whenever I tried to write an email or use my brain; it would turn into a strange feeling of resistance or recoil, but even if I wasn't doing anything, it would still consume me through the day as well as a strange foggy feeling. I felt disconnected from the rest of the world.

This made working incredibly difficult. Nic and my family were incredible at moving the business into a holding pattern and keeping it afloat at a bare minimum until I could return to work. I was also having regular crippling panic attacks, and they were far more physical than I ever realised: my hands would go numb and tingle, I'd experience tightness of breath and my heart would race to the point where I'd genuinely think I was having a heart attack. It was at this point that I first started seeing a psychologist on a weekly basis to get some help with rebuilding my mental resilience and learn how to manage my mental health.

Healing my mind was a much harder and painfully slower process than healing my body had been – for Nic, too, who was stuck between not knowing how to help and running our businesses and personal lives all by himself. It took weeks before I was able to start introducing a few emails or other forms of brain work and, for months after that, I'd take one step forward, two steps back: I'd work for a few minutes more than I could cope with and the next day, be stricken with paralysing anxiety again.

For someone who had learned to value themselves through the output of their brain and their ability to achieve things, I had never felt like such a failure; especially as I didn't know how long this would last or if I'd ever come through it. It took over six months of weekly work with a psychologist and barely any heavy brain lifting or socialising before I started to feel a bit normal again and over a year to get back to a point where I didn't relapse every few weeks.

For ages, I worried that I'd never be able to cope with a full life again, but what really helped me was my psychologist asking me to treat it like a physical injury. Physical rehab is intense and drastic while you heal, but once you've recovered, you need to take special care with that area in future but can generally return to normal. I had given myself an acute injury from overdoing *everything*, so I had to heal first and then go into maintenance mode. I love this analogy, because I think this is what leads us to under-estimate the importance of mental health; we can't *see* the impact of the injury like we can when we break a leg.

Since then and still now, my routine has changed drastic-ally to make space for my mental wellbeing and keep my anxiety at bay. I still meditate daily (sometimes twice), have much healthier limits on social interaction and mental stimulation each day and week (I've dubbed my Sundays, 'Sloth Sundays'), and I still see my psychologist regularly. Of course, there are still days when anxiety rears its monstrous head, and I still feel like a failure sometimes if I don't get the balance right, but I have *mostly* been able to rebuild a full and yay-filled life around my mental health. Now, I try to speak as openly as I can with others about my experiences to reassure them that if they are experiencing something similar, they can find their way through it – even if not in the same way that I have.

Slow down to speed up

These kinds of personal setbacks are alarmingly common among those of us who opt for a high-powered, jam-packed lifestyle. Our A-type drive can make it hard for us to pace ourselves and slow down. Even the great Arianna Huffington once found herself lying face-down on the floor in a pool of blood after collapsing from pure sleep deprivation and exhaustion before realising the importance of looking after herself. My friend Melissa Ambrosini, author of *Mastering Your Mean Girl*, was hospitalised after burning the candle at all ends in the name of her goals. Adrenal fatigue, thyroid problems, hormone imbalances, depression, an eating disorder and cold sores all over her face, mouth and down her throat stopped her in her tracks, but led to the reinvention of herself and her career. Motivation and drive can be powerful, even volatile, forces when things are going well, let alone when shit hits the fan and things start to fall apart.

 A huge part of seizing your yay is not just physically resting, but emotionally resting, too.

Hopefully, the more we all share our stories with each other, the more we can all appreciate how connected our minds and bodies are. A huge part of seizing your yay is not just physically resting, but emotionally resting, too. Pushing ourselves too far and too fast can have consequences that are equally as devastating and disheartening as financial and business-oriented setbacks – sometimes more so. If you are struggling to get back to what feels 'normal' for you, I encourage you to speak to your GP and ask for help – before things hit rock bottom, if you can.

Psychologists and other professionals don't wave magic wands at you; I see it as them providing valuable and practical tools to help extract the mess in your mind, untangle it and put it back in more neatly. Even though I don't have such an acute need for psychological support now, I still go back to therapy regularly as an investment in my mental endurance and it's one of the best hours spent in my week. Take comfort that there are lots of resources these days to help you recover such as Beyond Blue and Lifeline or psychologists. It's crucial that you use these in order to learn what you need to change in order to come back stronger and more equipped than ever for the next phase of your life.

An unattributed quote that I only found recently but have been in love with ever since is, 'Not all storms come to disrupt your life, some come to clear your path.' What a beautiful way to provide perspective and guidance to those who are in the middle of a shitstorm, be it professional or personal, wondering what on earth they did to deserve it and how they'll emerge intact. Even though it might feel like your world has been turned on its head and everything is going wrong, this moment can provide you with a wonderful opportunity to build things back up in the way you actually want them to be. I have heard many great stories of people starting businesses or making drastic life changes to allow them to flourish after being made redundant from their jobs. There are cases where there haven't necessarily been a failure or a situation that was going badly, but rather an unexpected storm that clears the way for something better.

Michael Ramsey always reminds me that if building dreams wasn't hard, everyone would do it. You have to be ready for all the shit bits as well as the great bits because they are all part of the package. The best way to arm yourself for this roller-coaster ride is to learn how to pick yourself back up and move your focus from the setback to the comeback as quickly as you can. Sometimes, this might involve seeking outside help (as I have), which I am so glad is becoming less stigmatised and I can't recommend highly enough. Other times, help might be closer to home. Remember the village you've been building, too; they're around you for a reason. There's no glory in being a lone wolf if reaching for help could get you there faster, better or healthier! Of course, give yourself the emotional breathing space to accept, reflect and ready yourself again (which could take a while depending on how drastic the fall), but then get back out there with a vengeance.

The comeback: how to put the pieces back together

The title of this chapter perfectly captures my attitude towards failure or setbacks these days. There are only two options: win or learn. Either things turn out wonderfully and exactly as you'd hoped (or better). Or, they don't turn out as well as you'd hoped, but you learn an incredibly important lesson for how to do things better next time.

While there is so much literature out there that teaches and guides us on ways to succeed, it is rarely acknowledged that there is an art to failure. So how exactly do we glean those lessons from what happened? The wisdom gained from failure is incontrovertible, but how to uncover that wisdom is the thing that is often skated over. I don't have all the answers; I'm simply going to share a few things that have helped me build more resilience in the face of setbacks and then helped me to move on as quickly as possible from them.

Like Lisa, when I experience a failure, the first thing I do is distinguish between what went right and what went wrong. There is definitely a very fine line between knowing when to call it quits and when to press on with some adjustments. It can be incredibly difficult to determine which route to take. Sadly, I think many people completely trash an idea when only a small part of it actually needs refining or changing. And sometimes, the actual idea or execution can be great, but bad timing or external factors out of your control lead to failure – meaning there's no reason *not* to try exactly the same idea again in different circumstances. In most cases, the lesson will simply reshape your path; it's just a matter of shaking off the hit to your pride and confidence to build up the courage to try again.

Like self-doubt, failure is a misleading killer of dreams because when something doesn't work out, we often see it as a total failure rather than a hint to make a subtle adjustment. This is why I think successful people aren't always the best in their field, they're the people who are best at failing and recovering. There are certainly times when you have reached a point where the best way forward is to call it on an idea and shift your focus, like Sir Richard did with Virgin Brides, Virgin Cola, Virgin Vodka, Virgin Cars ... the list goes on. And this doesn't necessarily have to be because of failure but rather a lifestyle choice.

 Successful people aren't always the best in their field, they're the people who are best at failing and recovering.

If your yay is no longer bringing you joy (I can think of several people who have recently closed their businesses because it no longer served them), then it's time to re-evaluate. If that thing is distracting you from the things that are going well and make you happy, it makes sense to cut your losses and put your energy where it will have the most impact. But that should be an absolute last-resort option when you've exhausted every possible way to improve, refine or adjust. You will either finally succeed or learn another invaluable lesson: failure is simply a bump in the road, not a stop sign.

If you're going through hell, keep going

Some 'hellish' situations count as setbacks to be learned from, while others tear through your life and cannot be explained with my theory of yay. I generally believe everything in life happens for a reason, but it's how we respond to the things that show up for us that determines how they play out in our life. The jigsaw pieces all make sense in the end, but of course, there are always going to be outliers – situations of grief and trauma that cannot be orientated within my understanding of the purpose of life. 'You win or you learn' doesn't account for the seriousness of things such as cancer, accidents or family violence. There are a host of things that can't simply be shaken off as lessons to be learned. If you are experiencing anything of the kind, there are many different resources and organisations you can go to for more professional and experienced support than I am able to offer here – I acknowledge that there are many situations this book has no answer for.

In those times of personal challenge, some people are hesitant to seek help because there can still be some stigma surrounding therapy and reaching out – though thankfully, this is less the case these days. Other people are hesitant because they think they can work through things themselves. I can't speak for everyone, but I believe there are situations that warrant specialised help and that we can benefit enormously from enlisting the expertise of a professional. If you're reading this and thinking that the decisions I managed to make and the personal revelations I had during this time sound unrealistic given what I was going through, bear in mind that these happened against the backdrop of a once-weekly appointment with my very experienced psychologist. Don't let your pride make you suffer alone and possibly worsen your suffering for no reason.

If you're still getting stuck wondering why things have happened to you, I can only say that you might not ever get an answer to that question. A quote I love, from the

2010 film adaptation of C.S. Lewis' *The Voyage of the Dawn Treader*, is one that always helps me in times of inexplicable trial: 'Hardships are often to prepare ordinary people for an extraordinary destiny.' It helps me focus not on trying to figure out why I'm experiencing the difficulty, but also on my capacity to move through it and onwards into the future. It moves my attention to what lies ahead and reminds me that it could be extraordinary once I get there. You are always far stronger than you think you are, even if tough times might knock the wind out of you. Everything in life is temporary and every storm does eventually pass.

CHAPTER 10

You won't do a good job if a good job is all you do

I have a confession: it didn't feel quite right leaving this part of the book until the end because the topic it covers – distinguishing between our work selves and our private selves – is the most important thing I want to impart to everyone who reads this book. But it made sense to place this chapter here so we could first walk through the earlier facets of seizing your yay and give context to this discussion before we got here.

The distinction between our professional or productive identities, on one hand, and our private identities, on the other, is so important to explore, especially because some of us have never made this distinction at all. We all have 'work selves' (or at least most of us do) but not all of us have cultivated the other parts of who we are (yet).

Leaving our private lives until last to discuss serves as a perfect illustration of how easily the personal can slip down our priority list and, sometimes, fall off the list altogether. When everything else is so much louder and demanding of our attention, it becomes easy to let our time and energy become wrapped up in examining and evaluating our working lives. We don't give nearly as much airtime to who we are outside of our productive output or what we 'do' – after all, we are human *beings* not human *doings*. We define ourselves and others, and we make sense of things based on our jobs and output, but that was never meant to be the totality of who we are.

The bulk of this book has been dedicated to discussing how to chase your goals and find your joy in relation to your working dreams (whether entrepreneurial or intra-preneurial), and that is absolutely a crucial part of creating a life you love given how much of our time is dedicated to working. However, earlier on I briefly touched on the idea that you don't necessarily need to find joy in your work. Joy can be found in hobbies or elsewhere, provided you're searching for it *somewhere* in your life. It's only recently that we seem to have adopted this societal belief that your work must excite you and be fulfilling in every single moment in order for it to be worthy of doing.

It's called work for a reason. Historically, this word has always been defined based more on effort expended or activity undertaken than on the subjective engagement or satisfaction of the worker. My grandparents would probably turn over in their graves to hear millennials (and, to be fair, other generational groups) turn down great job opportunities simply because they don't see them as being 'fun' or don't feel 'passionate' about the industry or what the job involves day-to-day (okay, that's a mass generalisation, but a common stereotype). I have worked since I was fourteen and legally allowed to, and I wasn't at all passionate about most of the jobs I had, but I accepted that I had to work to get the 'cash monies' to pay those bills, bills, bills.

 We define ourselves and others, and we make sense of things based on our jobs and output, but that was never meant to be the totality of who we are.

I will always remember turning to one of the amazing people on that Rwanda trip with us, Pat O'Callaghan, to chat about the many ways the trip was opening my eyes to greater purposes in my life besides corporate law. And I shared with him how I had started feeling a little lost even though I wasn't a year into full-time work. He wisely responded that perhaps we don't need to be passionate about our work, and that instead, our work can simply be a means for us to fund a lifestyle that makes room for passion elsewhere. I had never really considered that perspective until that moment, and it really helped me get through the next few years at the law firm without constantly questioning why I didn't feel completely engaged by everything I was doing.

Understandably, many people may choose to stay in jobs they don't necessarily adore because, on balance, that job provides enough money, opportunities, growth, stability, etc. for them to live a good life and still have time to find joy in other outlets. If you're an artist or creator, turning your talents or passions into a job with specific briefs and deadlines can kill the joy it brings you, so perhaps you would rather *not* make your talent your job as well. I've had friends who have taken a risk on their passion and made a big life change only to find out it wasn't what they thought it would be, and they'd rather go back to what they had. It turns out, the grass isn't always greener when you get to the other side.

In those cases, rather than finding their yay in their work, those people have simply turned to other things in their life that bring them joy. The great thing about feeling the yay is that it has flow-on effects that can filter through to all other areas of your life from just one activity that ignites you. I wonder if many people who feel unhappy at work are actually just unsatisfied generally in their life because they don't have a 'yay practice'. They're not investing any energy in finding that joy somewhere else, which could in turn make work tolerable – even enjoyable. It seems that, although I love the quote it came from, the essential element of seizing your yay *is not* just about finding a job you love and never feeling like you're working a day in your life. After all, I've been lucky to have found a job I love but some days definitely feel like hard work! Rather, seizing your yay is more about finding *something* you love and making time for it at all costs.

Even if you have been able to merge your passion with your profession, like I have, it is still crucial to distinguish between your work identity and your joy outside of that. You'd be forgiven for thinking your yay project was done, but work (even very happy, fulfilling work) was never meant to be the whole picture. In fact, in your situation, it's possibly even more important to draw a line between your life inside and outside of work because, when you're completely dedicated to and invigorated by your work, you have no motivation to stop or put boundaries in place, and can easily become consumed by it. When you're indifferent to or disinterested in your job, by contrast, that desperate desire to clock off and do other things helps make the distinction between work life and personal life much clearer.

 Frustratingly, I have realised that you can actually have too much of a good thing.

So now, whether you love your job or not, you can't do a good job if it's the only thing you do. We live in a 'more' society that conditions us to think that more is better, but I've found that all (or most) things are actually best in moderation. As you've heard, I had to learn this the hard way during my first few years in business. At first, my new job felt like pretend work because it was so much fun, so I never felt like I needed a break from it. That drive was fuelled by how visible the impact of our labour was on the growth of the business. Unlike my corporate job, I could see the direct financial and growth benefits when I worked longer and harder on our business, so what was my incentive to invest time in anything else?

You already know that this relentless mentality ended up in my complete physical burnout (again, the face-palming is real). But it also ended up in two other kinds of burnout that I hadn't encountered before: emotional and creative burnout. Frustratingly, I have realised that you can actually have too much of a good thing. Positive and exciting stimulation is still stimulation, and all of us need time out both physically and mentally. Everything works better when you unplug it for a break then plug it back in, including us.

Look after your body, it's the only place you have to live

It's fairly obvious that our body has physical limits, we're sometimes just not very good at identifying what those are until we've well and truly crossed them. Unless your job depends heavily on your physical state or performance, like in the case of elite athletes, many of us are quite out of touch with the impact of our lifestyle on our bodies. I know that I assumed that as my job wasn't physical it probably wasn't taking much of a physical toll on me. It took many a rude awakening and some serious symptoms before I realised that I'd been chipping away at my energy bank more than I thought, without taking the time to put deposits back in. I only learned my limits (and trust me, I'm still learning every day) by mistakenly crossing them and paying the price afterwards. It is so important to start learning the signs your body sends you when it needs you to take a break, and respect how important it is to respond effectively.

We ask so much of our bodies these days. We bombard them with information and sensory overload on the daily, then get frustrated when they won't keep up. I hope that you haven't had to experience a full health crash or burnout to fully grasp the importance of resting and taking breaks from work, although it wouldn't surprise me if many of you have. Even short of a full-health burnout, there can be so many other negative health or wellbeing outcomes that can happen when you don't look after yourself physically. For example, regularly catching colds and getting sick from low immunity is uncomfortable and inconvenient.

When I'm pushing it, my body's signature move is to flare up the old swollen glands down the sides of my neck and throat, and my immune system starts to fight back in response. If I ignore this for long enough, my body will whip out the beginnings of a delightful UTI (urinary tract infection), which is not a good time at all. For some of you, your body's messages may come via cold sores or mouth ulcers or whatever else your body does to show you it's on struggle street. It's funny how we think it's optional to slow down in those times rather than essential to do what our body is screaming for.

I have (I hope) gotten better at responding to these physical signs of being run-down before things get too serious, but I still grapple with that pesky little bugger, adrenaline. After moving into the health and wellness industry, I learned just how much you need to nurture your body and interpret the signs it so readily gives you about what it needs. But I'd wait to hear from my body before I'd slow down, rest or take time away from building the business. The problem with this approach was that adrenaline would creep in and gave me a false surge of energy and motivation – it would override any other symptoms my body might be giving me. This would keep me going well beyond the physical limits of my body, and before I'd know it, I'd have done too much damage.

Adrenaline can make you feel so good – like you're thriving and filled with unlimited energy – when you're really just entering the primal 'fight-or-flight' state traditionally reserved for dangerous or stressful situations. Now, I'm learning that I won't always *feel* like I need to rest before I truly need to because adrenaline can so cleverly mask the signs.

The science around our fight-or-flight response is fascinating. To put it simply, we are meant to spend most of our time in a normal, relaxed state sometimes referred to as 'rest-and-digest'. Occasionally, however, things around us that are threatening or terrifying will trigger a stress response known as fight-or-flight. When our ancestors confronted danger in their environment, they'd have one of two choices: stay to fight the danger or flee to escape it.

In a modern-day context, the trigger for a fight-or-flight response could be a physical threat such as a growling dog or the fear of a big presentation at work. It can even be a *perceived* fear, such as a phobia. When this response is triggered, the body prepares itself to react to danger and a flood of hormones activates the sympathetic nervous symptom, which then stimulates the adrenal glands to release adrenaline as well as other chemicals. When this happens, you might feel yourself becoming much more alert, your body tenses up and your heart rate increases.

This type of stress can be critical to our survival in a dangerous situation, and it can help us perform under pressure. The problem these days is that we are surrounded by so many potential triggers that we spend prolonged periods in this fight-or-flight state. We then mistake this for genuine energy without restoring the equilibrium of rest-and-digest. The productivity hamster wheel I speak of, and the constant stream of busyness, can leave us in a state of chronic low-level stress.

Before I understood this form of energy and alertness, I would mistake it for having a full tank of energy and I'd push through life at full speed (or in 'beast mode' as I love to call it). This unwittingly destructive pattern put my adrenals in overdrive and ultimately led to burnout. Nowadays, I am more conscious of focusing on restoring the rest-and-digest mode and returning to a tranquil, balanced state of mind as much as possible. This is one of the reasons I feel it's so important to give yourself time to *literally* slow down and rest, even if you don't necessarily feel like you need it just yet.

If you want to read more about this, I often turn to the work of Dr Libby Weaver, internationally acclaimed nutritional biochemist, author, speaker and founder of her own plant-based supplement range. One of her books, *Exhausted to Energized*, was especially helpful to me and helped me to understand my energy systems and ways to interrupt the burnout circuit. Although I have tried, unsuccessfully, Dr Libby explains that we cannot fight our biology and the symptoms that our body 'gifts' us to guide us towards the things our body needs more of. The key to better health is not resisting those signs and making better choices accordingly.

 Nowadays, I am more conscious of focusing on restoring the rest-and-digest mode and returning to a tranquil, balanced state of mind as much as possible.

To be clear before we go further, I am absolutely no stranger to the guilt and discomfort of slowing down something that is going well or that 'needs you'. It's not as easy as just pressing 'pause' on your life and responsibilities. In most situations in our modern-day life, the to-do list is never-ending because there's always something else we could be doing and the incentive to rest seems to get feebler every day. In the case of small-business owners, you are often the only person who can do most of the work so if you take time off, literally nothing gets done. If you're a parent, which I am not just yet but can fully appreciate, the guilt of taking time off rather than spending every spare minute with your family would be even more intense.

What keeps me focused in those times is to come back to the whole idea of reframing things in a way that gets the message through to your brain. For example, if you don't want to rest because you want to be productive, just flip that into a reminder that if you wipe yourself out and get sick, your productivity will stoop to a grand total of zero. In that light, it becomes irresponsible not to rest and pace yourself. Same goes for parents or anyone else, really. Remind yourself that there's no point going at 110 per cent of your capacity for a few days before crashing and making yourself useless, when you can go at 80 per cent and last forever. If your concern is that taking a break or looking after yourself takes time away from others, think of how crabby, exhausted or distracted you will be around them if you're unwell or exhausted.

Something that also comes to mind here is an anonymous quote, 'You are not required to set yourself on fire to keep others warm.' While some of us are prone to burn out through overwork or pushing too hard on our own way to yay, others burn out trying to help those around them at their own expense (or, if you're like me, a combination of both). Very early on when I started seeing my psychologist, the first word she introduced me to was 'enmeshment' which, on a technical level, is one of many schemas or patterns of thought we use to organise our understanding of the world and frame our thinking. (If you're interested in schema therapy, look it up. It will likely spark a lot of reflection.) Put simply, enmeshment describes excessive emotional involvement in the life of another (or, in my case, also in the wellbeing of our businesses), in which boundaries are permeable and unclear. After learning more about this, I recognised that this was a huge (and long-enduring) area of concern for me; I was constantly setting myself on fire for other people.

While I find it hard to rest at the best of times, I find it even harder to switch off to the needs of others. For example, I find it very hard to say no when people request a sit-down or a coffee so they can run through their business ideas because I genuinely get excited to help others succeed and want to pay it forward for those who helped me in the same way. I also think once we start to see ourselves as a type of person (e.g. a giver), we put so much pressure on ourselves to keep up with that standard (perhaps by going out of our way to keep giving at all costs). I would often commit to giving far more help than I was able to provide while also maintaining my own work *and* down-time. I intimately understand the guilt factor in saying no to people and how it can feel awkwardly selfish. But I'm slowly starting to understand that saying yes to others sometimes costs you what you need for yourself and it's not selfish to prioritise those things again so you show up better for those around you. Some might even say that self-care is a community service!

 You are not required to set yourself on fire to keep others warm.

Of all the things that will constantly change throughout your life – your location, your surroundings, your family, your friends, your job – the one thing you are stuck with, and the thing through which you *experience* that life, is your body. And yet, we so easily forget that and invest our time and energy in everything else. What you overdo now, you steal from later, and while it might not seem so in your younger, reckless days, physical health is a longevity game. In the more relevant present, the quality of your physical state is going to have an impact on the quality of everything you experience in that body. As an obvious example, you all know what it feels like to try to live your best life with a hangover. It's not exactly the best foundation for gratitude and zest for life.

Self-care is not selfish; it's imperative. The more your physical self is nurtured and well fuelled, the better the outcomes of your performance and emotional state will be (for you and the others around you). There is so much evidence about how important good nutrition and regular exercise are, and how they have positive effects on all areas of life. In my case, I have slowly been learning how to make my health a non-negotiable. I've been building certain things into my week to support myself in this area. I've learned that we are so incredibly different to each other, and things that work amazingly for some people will do nothing at all for others. It's a great thing that health and wellness is becoming a bigger industry, and that we have access to so much more information, but we are positively swimming in confusing and sometimes contradictory information. If you're interested in improving your health, I highly recommend seeing some experts who can tailor things to your body and lifestyle.

Broadly, what I think is most important to prioritising health is that you find some sort of routine that makes it easy for you to stay consistent. It's also important that you make decisions about this time for yourself in advance so you can't forget to factor it in. I'm constantly tweaking and adapting my personal routine, particularly between the seasons or between trips, but there are a few key things I try to keep up.

- **Exercise three–four times a week:** Like many of us, I've admittedly been through phases of working out every single day religiously, and I've overdone it without needing to. I didn't realise at the time, but my strict daily gym visits when I was working at the law firm were probably also motivated by my mental rather than physical needs, as they provided a midday break from whatever I was working on. Now, a daily workout is too ambitious for me given everything else I want to fit into my week without skipping any sleep. As we discussed above, my body's appearance isn't related to my job, so I don't need to prioritise working out over other activities that leave me feeling strong and balanced, although I completely understand that some of you may have different goals. After lots of experimentation, I have found that three–

four decent workouts of 30 minutes to an hour per week with a few gentler walks with our dog in between is a great balance for me. Any less than this and I feel sluggish or lethargic; any more and I start to feel quite run-down and perpetually sore. So, while some of you might thrive off a once-daily or even twice-daily form of movement or exercise, that frequency has the opposite effect on me and leaves me feeling *less* energised.

- **Experiment with different workout styles:** Like most things, it's good to move your body in different ways instead of repeating the same thing over and over. I'm a bit phase-y and find I get obsessed with something for a few months before swapping to something else. I've done yoga, F45 workouts and, more recently, running. But I also have a short attention span so when something becomes too predictable, I get bored and like to change it up. A typical week of workouts for me might include a weights session, a cardio workout like F45 or a long run, some conditioning like Pilates or yoga and then a repeat of something or a random fun class like boxing or something I haven't tried before. I'm quickly falling in love with the new Strong rowformer classes that Michael Ramsey recently brought to Australia. These combine the isometric conditioning of reformer Pilates with the intense cardio fitness required for rowing. When I'm travelling, I find it harder to keep up a routine, but I'll often take a resistance band with me and do a body-weight-resistance workout or just find a staircase to run up and down. Whatever form suits you, it's just important to move your body not only for your physical form but for the many mental benefits (love that rush of endorphins!).

- **Drink more water:** I've always been a relatively good water drinker, especially since my teen years when my skin was more temperamental. You probably know that water makes up around 70 per cent of our body composition, and that staying hydrated is vital for optimum functioning of every process within your body. Hydration affects our skin quality, body temperature, oxygen levels and our digestive system, among many other things. However, as Dr Libby explains in *Exhausted to Energized*, too many people live their lives in a constant of mild, chronic dehydration even if they are aware of how much of our body is water. If you're feeling foggy or fatigued, you might be overlooking hydration as a contributing factor when a simple glass of water could help you feel better. I try to drink two–three litres of water per day. Make it easier for yourself by keeping a nice water bottle or glass on your desk or wherever else is easily accessible so you can keep track of your intake throughout the day.

- **Eat plenty of wholefoods and very little processed foods:** I don't want to get too prescriptive here as I don't have a nutrition background and I know that we all function best with different nutritional regimens. There are some wonderful books out there that I regularly refer to for guidance in the food department, including books by Lola Berry, Luke Hines, Taline Gabriel and Lee Holmes. I don't subscribe to any special form of diet (although I've tried more than my fair share, none of which worked as well for me as intuitively eating), but I try to eat a lot of wholefoods, a small ratio of meat to plants and as few processed foods as possible. I generally eat three big meals a day with lots of snacks throughout to keep my energy sustained. I'm one of those very sensitive 'hangry hippos' who gets spacey and irritable if I go too long without food, so you can imagine how badly it went when I attempted intermittent fasting. When I'm working intensely, physically but also mentally, I go to town on snacks to fuel my brain – many a spoon of peanut butter was consumed straight from the tub in the writing of this book.

- **Get at least eight–ten hours of sleep:** The most easily sacrificed area of our physical wellbeing tends to be sleep, even though it is the one most directly related to our performance. How many times have you cut into your beauty sleep because of a deadline or a Netflix binge (or a big night out, if you're more of a party animal than me)? If you need any convincing on the importance of sleep, you must read Arianna Huffington's *The Sleep Revolution*, which collates all the knowledge and research on the benefits of sleep in the most digestible but action-provoking way. A statistic that still shocks me is the similarity between being drunk and pulling an all-nighter: a study in the *Occupational and Environmental Medicine* journal found that after 17 or 19 hours without sleep, participants performed worse than someone with a blood alcohol level of .05 per cent. Everyone has a different threshold when it comes to the amount of sleep they need to feel their best, and it can take a bit of trial and error to work out what yours is. It also changes with time; now that I'm over 30 my sleep needs are very different than they were when I was 20. Given all the adrenal fatigue in my history, my sleep requirements are higher than the average person, so I work best off a ten-hour sleep (and I still sleep-in on weekends). This just goes to show, you don't have to be a 5 am riser with a three-hour morning ritual to live a yay-filled life.

Whatever your threshold is, take the time to figure it out and stick to it. Since childhood, I've been a nightmare to get to sleep, even though I adore it once I finally wind down and let it envelop me. Poor Nic has to deal with making me wind down every night, knowing how ineffective I am when I don't get my eight to ten hours. Because I know I don't find it easy to let go of the excitement of the day, I've slowly developed a sleep routine to help signal to my mind that it's time to shut down. All the apps on my phone shut me out at around 8 pm, making it a big barrier to override that if I wanted to work/ scroll mindlessly later. There's an oil diffuser and silk mask next to my bed that physically cue me for sleep time. We all have different things that work for us. Of course, brand-new parents are the exception, I know they have few opportunities for a full night's sleep, but sleep will eventually find them again (although if I come back for a second book as a mum, I may revise that!).

  You don't have to be a 5 am riser with a three-hour morning ritual to live a yay-filled life.

Looking after yourself can seem overwhelming but you don't have to tackle every aspect of your wellbeing at the same time. It can be done in small increments, perhaps by starting with a little exercise and taking things from there. We often revert to the excuse of not having time, but you always have time for the things you put first. If you don't put your health first, how can you expect your body to give you the best results? There needs to be as much give as there is take, so make time to give back to yourself. And that doesn't just mean physically, but also mentally and emotionally. Finally, we've arrived at the wonderful topic of play!

CHAPTER 11

Play to yay!

While physical wellbeing and the risk of burnout is something that is more openly spoken about now, it's the emotional and creative burnout that really took me by surprise – I didn't even realise that was a thing on its own. Physical wellbeing is slightly more visible and measurable from the outside, but I had no tools to deal with feeling emotionally *and* creatively burned out, nor did I know how to refill those new cups.

By this point, I had come a long way from the superficial understanding I had of wellness back in the legal days. I had come to appreciate the vital importance of rest and was engaged in a sort of wellbeing balancing act between my work and physically resting to take care of myself (i.e. everything we just discussed above). But I still hadn't quite grasped one key factor; the thing I had missed in the work/rest linear equation was the third and most important element of that interaction. Enter the third major prong of seizing your yay, an oft-overlooked area of life: PLAY.

We aren't put on this beautiful earth to just work and die one day, there is a whole area of life I had forgotten all about and that's how to play. Just as our bodies can burn out and stop performing at their best, our minds are equally vulnerable to overwork and exhaustion. In my case, this was the severe bout of anxiety that accompanied my physical burnout during the second half of 2016, which advanced into depression a few times. I had never really experienced mental obstacles like these. I'd leaned heavily on my mental and emotional resources throughout my studies and during the start of my legal career, without ever appreciating that I had to refill that bank if it became depleted. I had no real strategies for recharging myself mentally or finding equilibrium again, nor did I really understand what I was experiencing.

As I've already mentioned, before I knew much about mental health, I'd hear about people with anxiety and wonder why they didn't just go and get a massage or take a beach holiday to chill the hell out. Now, I know it's definitely not that simple. The concepts of 'feeling anxious' and experiencing 'anxiety' are far more different than their names might suggest. You can only imagine the education that lay ahead of me when it came to understanding and implementing a mental and emotional aspect to my wellbeing routine. But once I started to, I was shocked that I'd managed to survive so long without one!

I have come to learn that my error when it came to my emotional and mental wellbeing was my understanding of stimulation. I was aware that prolonged stress, grief or other negative forms of mental stimulation could cause troublesome long-term effects, but I had to learn that you can also positively stimulate your brain too much and burn out its stores. Even positive stressors can trigger your 'fight-or-flight' response, especially when you start overdoing them without any downtime in between. Combined with my misinterpretation of adrenaline as energy, this was a recipe for disaster.

To restore myself, I was slowly coming to terms with the fact that I had to start saying no to things I didn't want to do. This may sound silly, but it seems like a lot of us have had to relearn this pattern. What really surprised me was that I also had to start limiting things I *wanted* to do – even if I felt like I had the energy for them. I was filling my schedule with things that I thought constituted 'downtime' but even those were a form of work or stimulation that was more depleting than replenishing. For example, yoga had been my preferred form of finding Zen and managing stress, but after starting Matcha Maiden, we began stocking our products in all our local yoga studios. Suddenly, the whole experience of visiting a yoga studio was turned into a work-brain-dominated activity.

This kind of cross messaging happened even when I thought I was fully immersed in self-care activities. I would set off for a relaxing walk and simultaneously tune into a podcast about financial growth or another topic that was heavy on the brain. This brings us back, again, to the productivity hamster wheel. My brain was so geared towards progress and achievement that I couldn't 'waste' any time. Even a relaxing, indulgent bubble bath had to be enjoyed while listening to something educational or developmental. I needed to be bettering myself or learning productively even while relaxing.

I therefore also had to learn to distinguish between activities that were 'not work' but still stimulating (i.e. listening to business podcasts or reading self-help books) and 'not-work' activities that were *replenishing* and unwinding (i.e. listening to a pop culture podcast or reading a fiction book). During that period in my life, I was also surprised to discover that I'm actually quite an introvert, and not the extrovert I'd always defined myself as. While I am extroverted in how I like to *spend* my energy – out and about surrounded by people – I am introverted in how I *recharge* that energy. I need complete distance from productivity, often alone, to coax my brain away from the to-do list. I had to unravel all that categorising in my mind of every activity into either the work or rest category (e.g. physically sleeping) and make a whole new *acceptable* way to spend my time doing things that had no productive outcome other than joy. That's where PLAY comes in.

Redefine your metrics for success

I don't think I realised it at the time, but I had two major revelations in Rwanda that have heavily informed the development of my philosophy of seizing the yay. Of course, the natural revelation for many after a charitable expedition to Africa is intense gratitude for the opportunities, safety and circumstances of their lives in the Western First World (made more poignant in my case because of my adoption). What I didn't expect was the simultaneous, almost opposite revelation that despite our privileged lives back home, I saw a purer happiness in the Rwandan children sparked by the few simple things they had than I saw in First-World communities.

How funny that I have had to do this much work to peel back all the layers of productivity and success and self-worth to rediscover what my natural state of yay is, when these children have known it all along. Looking around when I came back, I saw that the wealthiest and most 'successful' or 'busy' among us were most certainly not always the happiest, and the beautiful concept of play was nowhere to be seen. This is when I had to change the metrics I measured my life by because they had stopped me from valuing this whole area of activity. As Gary Vee said on our podcast episode, 'I'm on an incredible mission to redefine the North Star from financial success to a happiness metric. I really believe it can be achieved.'

So much of the yay-seizing for me has been about tweaking and refining the metrics by which I measure my life. Success and money, while desirable in many ways, are not a quick and easy shortcut to happiness; my podcast chat with Erin Deering, co-founder of Triangl Swimwear, really crystallised my beliefs about this. Not long before I spoke to Erin, Nic and I had discussed the adage 'money can't buy happiness' while reflecting on how our attitudes have changed over the years. We had decided that it was not necessarily true because money *can* certainly give you options to explore and enhance your happiness, but it's absolutely true that it can't *replace* finding happiness in other things.

In Erin's case, the success and growth of Triangl was so rapid that she barely had time to emotionally catch up or cultivate her relationship with happiness. She and her former partner and ex-AFL footballer, Craig Ellis, co-founded the business after their first date at a beach, for which Erin was unable to find any affordable, attractive swimwear. This frustration gave birth to the brand, which exploded almost instantly as they launched during the height of Instagram's viral support of e-commerce, and were further fuelled by high-profile customers like Kim Kardashian, Miley Cyrus and Kendall Jenner. Erin and Craig quit their jobs and moved to Hong Kong to be closer to their business's supply chain and get things off the ground.

They were at a point where their combined savings amounted to A$500 and were borrowing from friends to fund their production, but experienced extraordinary success when they switched from wholesale to a purely online retail model. The pair hit sales of A$5 million in their first year, rising to A$25 million in the second and A$45 million in the third. In one sense, this was the ultimate dream outcome, and they initially enjoyed the flashy cars, beautiful hotels and endless travel. However, the speed and scale of their lifestyle change overwhelmed Erin in a way that she found challenging to cope with.

They ultimately ended up separating, and Erin made the bold step a few years in to step out of the business to focus on finding herself again and working on her role as a mother to their two children. She very candidly shared the story of the complex relationship between money and success and happiness, and how those things don't always *feel* how you think they will. Her story and honest perspective were so profoundly interesting and were so well received by our audience on the podcast for the unique insight it offered into defining your metrics. I come back to Erin's words often when reflecting on how my metrics for measuring my life have changed.

Time you enjoy wasting is not wasted time

So, what does it look like when you redefine your metrics in practice? And once you're ready to make time for it, how do you find your play to yay? This is where those lists of things we talked about in chapter 8 return. When you identify your likes and dislikes, there will be likes that aren't relevant to your working life, and those are probably going to be insights that can help you find your hobbies.

When I was working in law, I actually forgot that people had hobbies outside of their work, and I certainly didn't have a clue what mine would be. The way I define a hobby or 'play to yay' activity now is to look at the activities that make you forget what time it is. What engrosses you so fully that you forget to check your phone or to look at the clock? You might end up with a list of tactile, manual tasks that are mutually exclusive to phone scrolling or laptop use – activities such as gardening, puzzles, pottery classes or golf. It's important for me that my hobbies don't have a productive outcome. That way, I won't try to alpha them into a work-like productivity challenge.

You might find out some weird, unexpected things about yourself through this process of listing your likes. You may also discover interests that don't correlate neatly to anything else about you. When I reflected on the shows I was binging on Netflix and the podcasts I like to listen to, I stumbled on a very strong interest for me: crime. And not just true crime, crime fiction and murder mysteries, but full-blown World War history and spy stories. For a very touchy-feely, yay-loving person, it seems incongruent that I would want to spend my free time learning about a serial killer or World War battle. Perhaps it's because these events feel so far removed from my day-to-day life that I find my mind becomes completely distracted.

For a while I reverted to overthinking, and I tried to figure out if there were any strange underlying reasons for this sinister interest or if I should stop watching such heavy material. But I've learned not to fight my brain and I've accepted that the more you find out about what works for you, the luckier you are to have found things that help you wind down happily. I have also re-discovered the joys of giant puzzles and gardening (although I'm not sure my garden enjoys it as much as I do). While my methods of relaxation are quite physically passive, Nic's are much more active. He finds it incredibly hard to sit still and is absolutely in clover with a gigantic 1000-piece set of LEGO or a trip to Bunnings to work out what handyman improvements he can make at home.

Some people lean towards much-less technically 'restful' forms of play, and sometimes these can include a side hustle or job. Gary Vee, for example, needs very little rest at all, so he finds playful offshoots within his existing business to be his outlet (outside that, he also gets a huge rush from trading baseball cards). A close friend who works alongside Nic in The Bushy Creative, Alan Horn Thomas, is a fabulous creative designer by trade but has just written and published his first crime novel because creative writing is his yay. And as you now know, Matcha Maiden started off as a hobby or side hustle for us, just for the joy of the experiment. As we are all so different, the possibilities for ways to play are infinite. The key is to start exploring and experimenting to see what lights you up the most.

Find your yay-mates

In the same way that you might have workout buddies, you might also find that you unwind best with certain friends. Obviously, if you're in a relationship, it's important for you to have individual forms of play as well as relaxing, joyful activities you can do together. Nic and I have developed a little tradition recently that we make time for no matter what else is going on: we like to lock ourselves into things to stop work getting in the way so we have chosen a few activities you can book tickets for in advance. The Melbourne Symphony Orchestra, for example, puts on amazing performances throughout the year where they screen a blockbuster film like *Harry Potter* or *Star Wars* and play the musical score live – it's positively magical.

Another joint activity that brings Nic and I so much yay is travel. Conveniently, it also happens to be an important way to step out of your comfort zone and gain inspiration for your next steps, which makes it easier for me to justify the time and money it can require. Unlike some hobbies, travel isn't something we can indulge in every single week (although how wonderful would that be), but is something that brings me immeasurable joy and happiness. If I had to describe when I was at my most relaxed, unburdened and purely contented, it would be while exploring a city and culture in a place I'd never been before. Studying languages is also thoroughly enjoyable to me, even if I'm not able to do it by immersion. Keeping up with the languages I have studied through language apps and resources is another thing I love doing in my free time.

Your friendship groups might also have group traditions or activities that keep you accountable when it comes to taking time for leisure. Kristina Karlsson is part of a book club with a wonderful group of women that meets up all over the world each year. Ang, Nic and I recently started taking gymnastics classes on Fridays to literally throw our bodies around like children and shake off the week. It's so liberating to turn up for something and have no pressure or even self-expectation to be good at it or improve week-to-week. We focus simply on having fun. How strange that we need accountability buddies to remind ourselves to have fun and enjoy our lives! But without them, we can find ourselves living a life with too much work, not enough yay.

Quiet play

Sometimes, and it often takes me a while to realise this, what I truly need is time with nothing much at all in my brain. When my anxiety became serious, in addition to introducing gentler play and seeing a psychologist, I also implemented quite a dedicated meditation practice. I had previously experimented with shorter-form meditation on a more casual basis using guided meditation apps or Spotify playlists when I was feeling flustered. *Smiling Mind* is a great app, if you're in the market for one, or you can join Dr Elise Bialylew's 'Mindful in May' movement.

At the beginning of 2018, I decided to make a more dedicated commitment and did my Vedic meditation training with the delightful Laura Poole over a few full days. This introduced me to a more structured, twice-daily routine of 20-minute unguided meditations based on the repetition of a personal mantra to take away the optional, casual nature of my practice. Vedic meditation has remained one of the most impactful tools in being able to sustain the crazy lifestyle we insist on living. I even have a specific spot to retreat to on our front balcony – an egg chair that Nic bought me for Christmas one year sits out there and I'll crawl into it whenever I need a bit of peace and distance.

Before the sceptics among you dismiss meditation as 'woo-woo' (I know some of you will because I did, too, once upon a time), there is an increasingly large body of scientific research on the benefits of meditation on the brain and body. I won't go into details here, but feel free to look it up. The greatest thing about meditating is that even if you keep having thoughts the whole way through (the human mind is never truly empty), you're not introducing any *new* thoughts into your mind and are thereby allowing it to catch up to itself. You don't even have to believe it's working for it to actually be working.

I have a theory that has absolutely no scientific backing (or at least I haven't gone to the trouble of finding it because I'm so sure it's true) but works in my head: up until recently, humans had always evolved at a pace that suited the evolution of our external world and circumstances. However, the technological age has sped up our lives dramatically, and information has become denser than our bodies have physically had time to adapt to; which in turn triggers our fight-or-flight response more regularly than our bodies are able to manage. I think this rapid and multi-directional assault on our bodies and brains by our newly sped-up environment is why mental illness, stress disorders and various other health issues are rife. We are all feeling the effects of constant connection and stimulation, which is why play, and especially quiet play, has never been more important.

Health considerations aside, another major benefit to giving your brain a big break from work with some play stems from getting some distance and perspective. It is often after Nic and I have a holiday or take time away from our work that we stumble upon our biggest creative breakthroughs because we have a fresh perspective and greater clarity. In 2018, Nic and I flew to Tasmania, taking our first break from work in over eight months and invited Ang to come along. After a week or so of off-road exploring, we climbed Cradle Mountain, and while standing on top of it, I was struck with the idea that Seize the Yay should take the form of a podcast. Within weeks of having this idea, I was on my way to recording my first episode. This is just one of many examples of fresh, new ideas hitting me after a few days of space and distance from the daily grind.

You can't see the big picture when you're focusing on the smaller details, and there's nothing quite like stepping back to help you see things through fresh eyes. No joke, the great intellects of the world are known for having naps and breaking up their creative day to find inspiration. Famous micro-nappers include Albert Einstein, Leonardo Da Vinci and Salvador Dalí. And in a modern context, employees at Google, NASA, Samsung and other innovative companies are even able to access sleep pods so they can take naps, thereby boosting their overall productivity. Winston Churchill once said, 'You must sleep sometime between lunch and dinner, and no halfway measures. Take off your clothes and get into bed. That's what I always do. Don't think you will be doing less work because you sleep during the day. That's a foolish notion held by people who have no imaginations. You will be able to accomplish more. You get two days in one – well, at least one and a half.'

So many of the most successful people we hear of these days either have hobbies that are completely unrelated to their work or take regular holidays completely away from their daily life. They *make time* for those things despite their jam-packed schedules. Admittedly some people need less time off than others, and some hobbies might be a little less nap-like, but they still provide a brain break from the daily grind. During his time as the boss of Microsoft, Bill Gates started famously heading off for solo weeks at a cabin in the woods, and these became known as his 'think weeks'. Similarly, my friends Samantha Gash and Kemi, who I've mentioned, set aside time for 'thought showers' where they make space in their calendars to discuss ideas, projects, and things outside of the day-to-day. The first time I heard about this tradition, I went for a whole day believing they jumped in the shower together to let the running water provoke the free-flowing of ideas between them (I'm book smart but a little street dumb).

As well as the many ways he is inspiring, Sir Richard reaffirmed all the thinking I was doing on the importance of play during our time on Necker Island with Business Chicks. At the beginning of the book, I promised you that I'd come back to the bachelorette party he threw me, and it is one of the many examples of how he prioritises play between his hustling. Despite a schedule far more jam-packed than most in the world, he vocally encourages his staff and guests to make time for fun. Since my visit coincided with the last week before our wedding, some of the lovely guests colluded with Sir Richard to hold some bachelorette festivities including a 'toilet paper dress game' which involves teams creating the best makeshift dress out of toilet paper. Not only was I surprised that he made time to attend in the middle of the day but he even volunteered to be my rival bride, allowing the opposing team to wrap him up in a toilet paper dress before donning some of his wife's lipstick and walking down the aisle with me so we could find out the winner. He stayed out later than I did most nights and always showed up for a dance, a chat or a solid chuckle on all manner of topics.

Hooray for small yays

Aside from hobbies and activities, there are plenty of other things in your life that can bring you yay and help you feel your best. One thing that has become a non-negotiable for me is my daily morning breakfast ritual – a little date with myself. While I am quite capable of making the same breakfast at home that I pay for at a café (as Nic gently reminds me), I have finally dropped the money guilt and accepted that this is my happiest way to start the day. It gets me up and out of the house, I start the day with a big, nourishing breakfast to fuel my brain and body, and it provides me with a lovely few hours to myself where I can go through my emails and get a mental picture of the day ahead before I jump into the chaos.

It all comes back to just knowing yourself and owning what works for you. I am not a big fashionista or beauty nut, so the money I don't spend in those areas is redirected to my breakfasts. I'm basically *making* money by replacing all those unpurchased handbags with breakfast outings instead (or am I stretching that a bit far?). You might be the complete opposite and find that splashing out on a new skin product or pair of shoes gives you a little rush. Yay doesn't have to be material but it absolutely can be. And, of course, you don't want to go too overboard on any one thing, but there's nothing wrong with budgeting to prioritise the things that light you up.

Defend your non-negotiables

Given that looking after our physical health often takes a back seat when things get busy, play time is even more at risk of falling to the bottom of the list. But, at least in my experience, since putting my physical and emotional health first (hence making them non-negotiable), everything else in my life has benefitted enormously. If anything, I've been able to achieve bigger, brighter things because of this.

From a practical standpoint, like many other areas of my life, I find the most effective way to ensure I prioritise my wellbeing and resist the pull of the to-do list is to make it as easy as I can to stay on track, while making it as hard as possible to wander off-course. I do this by coming back to the benefits of setting some routine and boundaries. While used too rigidly, routines and boundaries can keep you too confined, but they can also be used effectively to help you defend your time.

One strategy to do this is to lay out your week, month or even year, and then start planning by carving out time for the things that are important for your physical and mental health in the same way you would for a meeting or trip that can't be shifted. This signals to you psychologically as well as visually that these things are of the utmost importance.

This diary can be a physical or digital one; it can even be a to-do list on a scrap piece of paper. It's treating your priorities as a formal appointment with yourself that is the key. Though I have largely let my colour-coding and alphabetising tendencies take a back seat, they come out in full organisational force when it comes to time management. We all have such a limited amount of time and so many things pulling our attention in different directions. If we don't plan, it's easy to end up at the weekend realising you spent all your time that week on things that *weren't* your priorities. This is the kind of 'busy' that isn't productive because it doesn't have any real direction.

When the important things are already blocked out before you start adding more things to your list, it's harder not to give them your attention. At the start of each week, I diarise absolutely everything that I want to get done throughout the week, month or year, and I put all my non work-related priorities into my diary at the *same* level of importance as my work tasks. This includes exercise sessions, meditations and catch-ups with friends. If I'm too casual about things and only commit my wellbeing blocks to my memory (like I used to), they can too easily get swept away in the mental hurricane of each day. It might sound silly, but this way it's harder for me to overestimate how much time I have and overbook myself like I used to.

My calendar ends up looking a bit like an old-school Tetris game, but that's exactly what the art of time management is about: squeezing a lot of strangely shaped, sometimes conflicting, multi-coloured tasks and events into the limited number of precious hours called life. The beauty of visually recording things as blocks of time is that if something comes up last-minute and you need to change your plans, you are prompted to *move* that non-negotiable somewhere else rather than scrap it all together.

Another valuable skill my mum taught me along with her crossroads-decision-making tools is the urgent–important matrix for prioritising tasks. Things that are urgent sometimes obscure the important because they're shouting more loudly at you. In order to uncover the true priorities, I divide a piece of paper into four and label each of the four squares: urgent–important, urgent–unimportant, not urgent–important and not urgent–unimportant. Then, I assign a task to whichever square suits it. This can be a very useful tool when you're really jammed on time and don't know what to attack first.

This exact approach might not work for you, but the point I'm making is that it's well worth your while to work out a way that *does* best keep you on track and encourages you to fit everything in your life *around* your non-negotiables. It doesn't have to look anything like anyone else's schedule, provided it results in the best version of you. I block out the whole of each Sunday because I can't manage my anxiety or function effectively without an entire day of hardly any stimulation each week. You know now that I call these my 'Sloth Sundays' because my goal is to move as little as I can.

I can squeeze almost anything into the week and even push the boundaries of my energy a little, as long as I strictly limit myself on Sundays and indulge in crime books, trashy Netflix shows, playing with the dog or going for a road trip. I sometimes feel like I'm a very lazy person living inside a very driven, activity-loving person's body – it's a bit confusing. Others might need a whole weekend to recharge, while, on the other hand, I have friends who don't really need much downtime at all. As long as you find your own play to yay, you're on the right track.

The magical art of saying nay

Once you've laid out the framework of your week and slotted everything into it (neatly, and in the right colours), the hardest part is then *defending* the structure you've created. Since I love stationery and organising so much (in another life, I could have been an executive assistant), learning to block out my calendar was the easy part. The much harder part, and one I know I'm not the alone in struggling with, is saying no to things that clash with those boundaries that I've set up – you're not really making something a priority if you let other things keep pushing it back. Unfortunately, getting a grip on using 'no' effectively is really the only way to honour what you need to feel your best.

Trust me, I have tried my very hardest to find other ways because 'no' is my least favourite word to use in the world, especially if it becomes confrontational in any way. But, if we come back to our yay frame and the ways we can redefine situations to make them easier for us to adapt to, it becomes clearer that every time you say yes to someone else's needs, you're often saying no to your own. 'Yes' is not a cost-neutral word you can bandy around, because it involves giving up some of your precious time. Once I started to understand this exchange of energy more clearly, I felt less guilty about using no to protect the things I need to feel my best.

Having really focused on carving out time for the things I've learned that I need in my week, I only learned through repeated, incredulous frustration at myself how bad I am at saying no. In fact, it took me several years of ending up in situations that I really didn't want to be in to realise that I was the one who had made the decision to be there earlier.

I kept wondering how, after doing all the groundwork on my calendar, I still did not have enough time for the basic things I needed to feel good. I have learned that you not only have to get comfortable with saying no, you also have to be ready to use it regularly to defend your time, energy and wellbeing. I began honing this 'no' skill by turning down the propositions or events that I already knew I didn't want to attend. Seems easy enough when you break it down. But when I still ended up feeling flustered and pressed for time every week, I realised that I also had to start saying no to things I *really* wanted to do but that just didn't fit within the framework of my basic needs. Hence why they are my non-negotiables.

It's a beautiful blessing to have more good opportunities than you can physically fit into your life, but it's also a true challenge, and one that you're likely to face once you start seizing your yay. But, if you think about it, every successful and fulfilled person out there must at some point have learned how to discern what the right opportunities are and say no to everything else. As Mark Manson elucidates in *The Subtle Art of Not Giving A F*ck*, the act of choosing a value for yourself requires rejecting alternative values. Returning to his signature bold profanity to hammer the point home, we all must give a fuck about something that we value, which necessarily means rejecting what is *not* that something. Getting our heads around this kind of rejection and saying no can make our relationships better and our emotional lives healthier. Just remember when it gets tough, you're still saying yes to the things you value.

Crafting your perfect no

While I've hardened up in some important ways, I refuse to let the fluffy get bashed out of me completely. I'm slowly getting better at initiating harder conversations, but fortunately (or unfortunately for Mark Manson), I'm still in the business of giving fucks about stuff. For those of you like me, it's important to remember that 'no' can be delivered gently and with compassion; it doesn't have to be blunt or aggressive to have the same result. There are always ways you can craft your delivery without hurting anyone's feelings.

If you find having these conversations hard, try offering some context or an explanation that might help the other person understand your no and not take it personally. I've gone so far as to draft templates for gentle rejections that strike a balance between firm and friendly that I'm comfortable with to respond to requests I receive more commonly than others. This saves me from having to make the emotional effort and concern of writing it from scratch each time, and it stops me saying yes just to avoid having to write the email, which I used to do. Most people intimately understand the paucity of time – people tend to respect you more for being clear from the beginning. Saying yes and stringing them along until you realise you've overcommitted or doing a terrible job is far less easy to swallow.

If you really don't want to shut the door on something completely, there are ways you can get around giving a definitive no without compromising on your boundaries. This murky area is a much more recent discovery for me. A key example of it in action are those situations where a 'quick coffee' or a meeting could be a simple email or a call. It's so much harder to make yourself physically available to someone; that entails getting ready, combating travel time, parking and all the other reasons it might be hard to leave the house. It is not as difficult, though, to squeeze in a chat on the phone.

When someone I don't know well or at all asks for help or advice, I often propose an email as an alternative to a physical chat. That way, I can still provide as much help or advice as I can, but I can do it on my own time, and in my pyjamas or in the various other less-than-presentable states in which I spend most of my time when I'm not meeting new people. Sometimes, that's as good as a 'yes' to the person asking. More often than not, I also approach their questions with a clearer, more patient head because I've been able to choose when I tackle them.

But, of course, there are also times where you simply don't want to do something or go somewhere for no special reason – you don't have to be defending a non-negotiable to have the right to say no. Surprisingly, while it's a good thing to be a good person, you don't in fact owe it to other people to offer them parts of yourself (except in certain, limited circumstances like baby showers or family obligations). I'm so very grateful to the many, many people who have nonetheless given me their time or energy before there was any inclination it would be worth their while or even enjoyable, and for that reason, I try not to ever be too guarded. As I often say, though, on rare occasions it's just too 'people-y' out there or I straight up CBF (you can figure that one out, I'm sure) and I've been slowly learning not to ignore those feelings and give myself some space.

Sometimes, Sloth Sunday hits on a weekday (especially at certain times of the month). You might be preoccupied with something as mundane as a Netflix series that you're thoroughly enjoying and feel you need to finish as an urgent priority. It took me well into my adult life to realise that you don't have to justify the way you spend your own time to anyone else. No is the most powerful you tool you have for ensuring your time is as yay-filled as it can possibly be.

Contribute to the collective yay

I sometimes get so caught up in the immense challenge of just working, living, feeling happy, staying healthy and doing all the things that I forget the broader legacy piece. Not everything we do in our life should be about us seizing our own yay. I couldn't finish the book without mentioning that, sometimes, we need to look at the collective and consider the overall yay of humanity. We spoke extensively about this on Necker Island: how we get very caught up in what feels important right now, and don't stop to think about our contribution to the future. This really opened my eyes to the fact that our legacy is the footprint we leave on this earth. I would never want that to simply be that I just lived a great life within my own little bubble.

Everyone will interpret their legacy differently, and philanthropy is not for everyone, but I think it's incredibly important to give back to your community and those less fortunate where you can, if you're so inclined. This might be done through contributing to a formal charity or even just a one-on-one relationship you have with someone, but there is nothing quite as rewarding as impacting someone else's life positively. A quote I love (based on a similar sentiment by Malcolm S. Ford) is, 'Character is how you treat someone who can do nothing for you.' While philanthropy is often understood as large-scale financial donations made by wealthy people to those less privileged or to an important cause, I think anyone can create a legacy in the way they treat others who aren't in any way connected with your own way to yay.

Sir Richard Branson is as passionate about making change in the social sector as he is in the business sector, and he shares his wealth generously to help many different causes. The majority of Richard's time is now spent on philanthropic efforts with Virgin Unite, his non-profit foundation build over the past 15 years. He covers all of its overheads, ensuring 100 per cent of all donations received go directly to where it is needed most, from health to human rights to tackling the climate crisis. In addition, 100 per cent of all the money he makes from speaking engagements, plus further donations made from Virgin Group, goes directly to Virgin Unite.

I wanted to ask Sir Richard what he thought we could do in our lives to be of service, and I used a quote to frame the question (no surprises there): 'If you cannot do big things, do small things in a big way.' When looking at how many important, worthy causes could benefit from our time and resources, I often find myself facing action paralysis.

Sir Richard's answer was incredibly interesting. He started by reminding us first to look after ourselves so that we are in a state to be able to help others – makes sense. Next, he talked about widening the circle to make sure you're helping your family and friends. Then, you might be able to help an old lady across the street and look more broadly at the community around you. As your business and influence grows bigger, you will then be able to tackle bigger and more complex things. You don't start as a global business or world leader, so you don't have to widen the net to the globe straight away to be making an impact. He also reminded us that we all have the power to call on influential people to pay attention to things we are passionate about. You might call 20 or 30 different people and face several hang-ups or rejections, but eventually you'll get through to someone and start from there.

I find immense joy and transformation in physically volunteering my time or donating resources to different causes, and Nic and I regularly do this where we can.

In my legal days, I volunteered for community legal clinics and crisis centres, and as a businesswoman, I support lots of different charities either as an ambassador or by helping raise awareness through other ways. In *Wake Up to the Joy of You*, Agapi Stassinopoulos says that the quickest way to feel like you are fulfilled and rich is to use your energy and natural talents to contribute to someone else's life. Importantly, you don't have to go to Africa to build schools or feed the homeless in your city or leave your life to join the Peace Corps (although they are perfectly honourable things to do if they suit you). Something as small as covering the cost of someone's coffee or offering a compliment to a stranger can brighten both of your days. There are some beautiful lists circulating on the internet of ways that strangers pay kindness forward that you could take inspiration from – they bring me great joy and laughter on a rainy day.

CHAPTER 12

Yay is a journey, not a destination

If you conceived of your way to yay as somewhat of a straight line when you picked up this book, I hope you are now able to see it as more of a chaotic scribble meandering all over the page. Importantly, I hope that you aren't disturbed by this change in perspective. Instead, I hope you find it reassuring to know that a happy, fulfilling life simply isn't meant to be straightforward or one-dimensional. The more tangents you have been off on along the way, the more well-rounded and open-minded you are likely to have become. The more tumbles you have endured and survived, the more resilience you are likely to have developed. And the more you can objectively evaluate and correct the course of that scribble as it advances across your page, the more you are likely to be able to adapt to change.

I truly believe that everything happens for a reason, but I also believe these happenings are subject to our own choices and control, provided we are brave and supported enough to exercise them. Each of us is constantly evolving, as is the world around us – at a pace that is faster and more overwhelming every day. We tend to search for one static moment of fulfilment and happiness, forgetting that it is the journey to get there that makes it beautiful.

We measure our lives against predetermined metrics based on amassing money or ticking boxes of 'success' while forgetting how to find comfort and satisfaction in play or pure stillness. We merge 'want' with 'should' and forget how to identify those moments we are invigorated or completely unstimulated. We glorify being busy then feel guilty when we do the basic things our bodies and minds need to thrive. There are many forces at work in our lives that can make it very difficult to focus on what truly lights you up, but if you are prepared to do the work and take the time to peel back the layers, it is not impossible to do this.

Seizing your yay turns the spotlight back on pure joy and happiness. It restores parts of the unburdened childlike sense of wonder that we somehow let go of as we grow older. I hope that this book, or at least parts of it, have provided a gentle push closer to that delightful sense of joy for your wonderful life. I hope I've encouraged you to start thinking about the way *you* are thinking in positive ways.

I sometimes feel like I've fully come into my own and started on the pathway I was born for, but simply beginning the process of writing this book put so many of the lessons I've shared in these pages to the test all over again. Writing, and eventually finishing, this book involved even more profound learnings than I anticipated – of old lessons and brand-new ones.

I've remembered how much joy I get from writing. I've realised how quickly self-deprecation and the throes of doubt can creep back, how I have more to say than I thought I did and how my philosophy has become deeper and more developed than I even realised. Reflecting on my village has made me grateful all over again for the many incredible humans I am lucky to be surrounded by, and how much they have impacted who and where I am today. I've realised how many different phases I have gone through, not just in the years since launching our businesses but also in my life to date, and how each of those phases has left me with something important – a lesson, a friend, a new tool. I have been reminded that this is an ongoing journey and not a destination.

To quote Einstein and finish on a high, 'No problem can be solved from the same level of consciousness that created it.'

Ultimately, every part of your life will *and should* look different from anyone else's. What works best for each of us is such a personal, unique thing to decipher and, as in my case, doing this can take quite some time and deep metacognition.

You might need to lean on your yay-bourhood at times, for a hug, a stomp or a shoulder to cry on. Other times, you might need to put on some heavy blinkers or journal aggressively to get you through some challenging and confusing times. You may veer towards or away from your yay over and over throughout the process of finding it as you experiment and navigate. It doesn't matter what your ultimate destination turns out to be so long as you remember to find some yay in the journey.

Thanks

Although you can tell by now that 'impossible' isn't a state of affairs that I'll accept lightly, listing all the people to whom I am grateful and/or indebted for the role they have played in this book and/or my life comes pretty close.

As well as the wonderful people who have been named throughout the book, I'd like to express my most heartfelt thanks to the following others (and many, many more) for their friendship, support and the many different ways they've shown me love:

Murdoch Books – particularly Kelly, Katie, Justin, Vivien and Lisa, for making this book a reality and working so hard to bring it to life

Genevieve Day – my wonderful manager who dedicated herself to getting this book published and who is always in our corner helping build our careers

Kat Karabatos, Laura Trimble-Thompson, Maire Lynch and Elizabeth Brant – my dear fellow nerdy Mac

Rob girls who keep my brain and heart stimulated

Vanessa O'Connor – my oldest and dearest friend

Yvette Arnott – my VCE English teacher who rekindled my long-lost love for writing

Colin Campbell – my law lecturer, thesis supervisor
and mentor from Monash University
My dad, Bill Holloway, his sister (and my wonderful
Aunty) Peg and our Gippsland family
Margaret Gearon – who gave me my love of all
things French
Peter Stirling and my other colleagues at King &
Wood Mallesons, for the best start to working
life that I could have asked for

And in no particular order:
Natalie Devitsakis, Colette Mintz, Nita Rao, Michael
Beaconsfield, Eliza Hilmer, Heba Kanjo, Kavisha
Kurukulusuriya, Mathika Perera, Jeanette Horn Thomas,
Jimmy Riedel, Chris Cavanagh, Katherine Roan, Ina Odak,
Danielle Glover, Attil Filippelli, Marc Champagne, Pauline
Latour, Megumi Ogawa, Rachel Swan, Susie Nguyen, Matt
Wood, Chris Maisano, Rachel Kelly, Josh Kaplan and the
many other people who have filled my life with yay.

Podcast Guests

The following are guests featured on the Seize the Yay
podcast not otherwise mentioned in the book

1. Osher Günsberg
2. Tim Robards
3. Danny Kennedy
4. Dany Milham
5. Elyse Knowles
6. Janine Allis
7. Eleanor Pendleton
8. Michelle Battersby
9. Georgia Love and Lee Elliott
10. Khanh Ong
11. Jane Lu
12. Daniel Flynn
13. Elyse Bialylew
14. Pana Barbounis
15. Jessica Sepel
16. Megan Gale
17. Rachel Kelly
18. Tiff Hall
19. Kat Stewart
20. Scott Henderson
21. Miki Agrawal
22. Jesinta Franklin
23. Emma Lewis
24. Sarah Hamilton
25. Gary Vaynerchuk
26. Melanie Gleeson
27. Dr Nikki Stamp
28. Olympia Valance
29. Amy Kate Isaacs
30. Renée Bargh
31. Priscilla Hajiantoni
32. Lincoln Younes
33. Chloe Szep and Molly Jane
34. Jeremy Muijs
35. Cameron Cranley
36. Guy and Jules Sebastian
37. Miranda Kerr
38. Dr Samantha Nutt
39. Sharna Burgess
40. Dominique Cotte
41. Madison de Rozario
42. Gemma Watts
43. Moana Hope
44. Harlan Coben
45. Abbey Way
46. Lana Wilkinson
47. Jake Edwards
48. Tasia Valenza
49. Wim Hof
50. Nicole Liu
51. Jasmine Smith
52. Dr Kieran Kennedy
53. Elle Halliwell
54. Mark Manson

References

Body Image Movement (movement/website)

Collective Hub (website)

Dream Life Journal (Kikki.K) by Kristina Karlsson

Embrace by Taryn Brumfitt (documentary)

Exhausted to Energized: Dr Libby's guide to living your life with more energy by Dr Libby Weaver

Finding My Virginity by Richard Branson

Happy, Healthy, Strong: How to feel amazing every day by Rachael Finch

Lean In: Women, work and the will to lead by Sheryl Sandberg

Mastering Your Mean Girl: The no-bs guide to silencing your inner critic and becoming wildly wealthy, fabulously healthy, and bursting with love by Melissa Ambrosini

Men Are from Mars, Women Are from Venus: The classic guide to understanding the opposite sex by John Gray

Mindful in May (movement/website)

Nice Girls Don't Get the Corner Office: Unconscious mistakes women make that sabotage their careers by Lois Frankel PhD

Risk & Resilience: Breaking and remaking a brand by Lisa Messenger

Seize the Yay (podcast)

Shameless (podcast)

Smiling Mind (app)

The Beauty Chef (website/blog)

The Essence of You and Me: An inspiring and heartwarming true story of resilience, hope and love by Kada Miller and Barney Miller

The Fit Foodie (blog)

REFERENCES

The Fit Foodie Meal Prep Plan: Easy steps to fill your fridge for the week
by Sally O'Neil

The Five Love Languages: How to express heartfelt commitment to your mate
by Gary Chapman

The Life-Changing Magic of Not Giving A F**k by Sarah Knight

The Sleep Revolution: Transforming your life, one night at a time
by Arianna Huffington

*The Subtle Art of Not Giving A F*ck: A counterintuitive approach to living a
good life* by Mark Manson

Thrive Global (website)

*Thrive: The third metric to redefining success and creating a life of well-being,
wisdom, and wonder* by Arianna Huffington

*Wake Up to the Joy of You: 52 meditations and practices for a calmer, happier,
mindful life* by Agapi Stassinopoulos

Winging It by Emma Isaacs

*Your Dream Life Starts Here: Essential and simple steps to creating the life of
your dreams (Kikki.K)* by Kristina Karlsson